Happy Birthday

For one of my favorites —
Sylvia —
        Love,
        Francine

6/2002

READER'S DIGEST

Fast & Fabulous

The Decorated Table

READER'S DIGEST

Fast & Fabulous

The Decorated Table

By the editors of *Handcraft Illustrated* magazine

The Reader's Digest Association, Inc.

Pleasantville, New York/Montreal

A Reader's Digest Book

Conceived and edited by the Editors of *Handcraft Illustrated*
Designed by Amy Klee

Library of Congress Cataloging in Publication Data
The decorated table / by the editors of Handcraft illustrated.
        p.   cm.—(Reader's Digest fast and fabulous)
    Includes index.
    ISBN 0-7621-0092-3
  1. Handicraft. 2. Table setting and decoration. 3. Tableware.
  I. Handcraft illustrated. II. Series: Fast and fabulous.
  TT157.D386 1998
  745.5—dc21   98-10221

Printed in the United States of America

Introduction

Whether styled with straight legs and a plain surface or loaded with ornate curlicues, a table is the perfect landscape on which we can play out our creative energies as crafters. This book is a collection of decorative projects that you can make and display on all types of tables—from the formal table in the dining room to the side table in the living room. These objects will always be a joy to look at, either from a slight distance as a passerby or at close range when you sit down to dinner. The scale of each project is small enough so it can be made on the kitchen table, and the materials are easy to find—many may not even require a trip to the store. I think you'll be pleasantly surprised at how easily you can achieve great results.

Chapter One, Table Accents, is a showcase for small touches that can bring a sense of style and tradition to your celebrations. A beautiful garland of roses made from ordinary crepe paper can enhance a dinner party of close friends, while a wheat sheaf made by binding dried stems around an aluminum can serve as a traditional autumn centerpiece. For your holiday table setting, you can make up a set of traditional Christmas crackers to use as party favors in about an hour's time.

Chapter Two, Table Lighting, features candles and candlesticks as well as projects designed for use with candles, such as a mosaic hurricane chimney and a votive candle townscape. Each of these projects will let you create dramatic, beautiful, and unique lighting for your tables—whether that constitutes a formal table setting, a holiday sideboard arrangement, or a solitary bedroom nightstand—in just a few easy steps.

In Chapter Three, Tableware, you'll be introduced to an assortment of stylish and graceful place setting ideas, including etched tumblers and martini glasses, hand-painted plates with modern designs, and silver leaf napkin rings made from curtain rings.

I have one wish with this book: that it provides you with everything you need for producing decorative pieces that you are proud of. In this regard, the full-color photographs, the step-by-step directions, and the hand-drawn illustrations are designed to support you every step of the way. And, if you are so inspired, adapt each project's materials and style to suit your own taste and make each project your own.

Carol Endler Sterbenz
Editor, Handcraft Illustrated

Contents

Table Lighting

Appendix

table accents

Victorian Spring Basket with Waxed Flowers

This spring basket, which imitates the porcelain baskets of England and France, is a fresh approach to the pretty but predictable Easter baskets. The porcelain effect comes from the Victorian technique of waxing roses, a simple process that you can do on your own stovetop. To quick-preserve the roses, dip them into a pot of melted paraffin, then gently lower them into a coldwater bath. The wax will harden within a minute; in twenty minutes you'll be ready to wire the flowers to a decorative basket. Waxed roses hold their color for about two weeks before turning brown.

———

We decorated this basket with light pink and yellow waxed roses. Within a few hours of waxing, the edges will brown slightly, giving the roses the look of antique velvet. For a more dramatic look, use a green basket and darker roses.

MATERIALS

- **Basket with handle**
- **Six medium pink roses with leaves**
- **Six medium yellow roses with leaves**
- **Four pink rose buds**
- **1yd (1m) 1½in (3.7cm)-wide white velvet ribbon**
- **Three blocks (1lb or 400g) household paraffin wax**
- **Spooled thin floral wire**
- **White thread**
- **Green floral tape**

YOU'LL ALSO NEED:

empty 16oz (500ml) can; 1qt (1L) saucepan; stove; knife; cutting board; chopstick; jar of water; deep bowl of cold water; pruning shears; waxed paper; two empty cereal or cracker boxes; tape; ruler; small, sharp knife; scissors; tongs; needle; paperweight; and hot-glue gun.

DESIGNER'S TIP

For better wax coverage, dip the roses into the wax at a slight angle instead of straight down.

Instructions

1. Set up work area. Set up double boiler and work area near stove. To make stand to dry waxed roses, tape cereal box closed, lay flat, and make sixteen ½in (12mm) **X**-shaped cuts, 4in (10cm) apart, across top surface. Set cereal box aside. Lay sheet of waxed paper on counter. Using pruning shears, clip rose and bud stems 6in (15cm) below base of rose and set in jar of water. Clip and set aside four to six three-leaf clusters.

2. Wax roses and buds. Cut paraffin wax into ½in (12mm) pieces. Drop two-thirds of pieces into can, set can in saucepan, and add water to sauce pan until half full. Bring double-boiler water to boil, then reduce to simmer. Using chopstick, stir wax until liquefied. Drop in additional wax and melt until can is three-quarters full. Turn off heat. When water stops simmering, hold rose by stem and dip at slight angle into liquid wax, without touching rose to can. Hold for two to three seconds (see illustration A, facing page), then remove rose, dip into bowl of cold water, and lift out. Clip stem to 2in (5cm) and prop upright in stand (illustration B). Repeat to wax remaining roses and buds, reheating to liquefy paraffin whenever it becomes dense or cloudy. Remove double boiler from stove. Allow roses to harden for at least five to ten minutes. Dip each stem into warm wax to seal cut end (illustration C) and replace in stand. Let all roses harden twenty minutes.

3. Wax leaves. Reheat wax. Using tongs, dip leaf clusters into liquid wax, then lay on waxed paper to harden (illustration D).

4. Attach waxed roses to basket. Weight basket with paperweight. Wrap stems with floral tape. Wrap 3in (7.5cm) length of wire once around each rose stem and twist, then insert wire ends between basket slats near base of handle (illustration E). Pull roses snug against basket, and twist wires to secure. Wire leaves around roses and buds.

5. Attach ribbon decoration. Hand-tack tiny pleats every 3in (7.5cm) across width of white velvet ribbon. Starting at basket handle, hot-glue middle pleat to basket rim. Glue adjacent pleats around rim (illustration F). Trim ends and glue down.

Making the Spring Basket

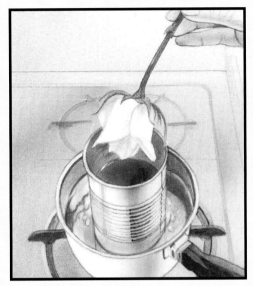

A. Dip each rose into the melted wax, then dip into cold water.

B. Trim each rose stem, then prop the rose upright in a cardboard stand.

C. Seal the cut ends of each rose stem by dipping it into the melted wax.

D. Dip the leaves into the melted wax, then dry them flat on waxed paper.

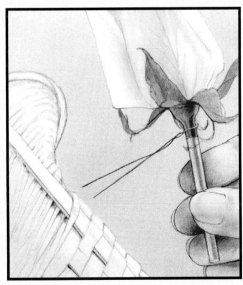

E. Attach the waxed roses to the basket with thin wire.

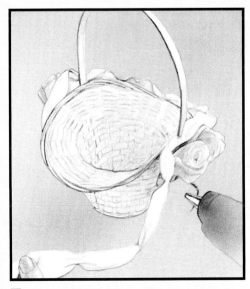

F. Hand-tack small pleats in the ribbon, then hot-glue it to the basket rim.

Rose Blossom Garland

Roses add romance, drama, and Victorian elegance to your home. With hand-made crepe paper roses, you can fashion a sweeping floral garland for a valance, mantel, or tabletop. Begin by creating the petals—the crepe paper's crinkly quality makes it easy to shape three-dimensional forms, and its sheerness simulates the look of real petals. Next, intermix your roses with store-bought artificial roses. Finally, attach them to a garland vine, and you'll have lifelike blossoms that will enhance any space.

—

The large crepe paper roses on this garland measure about 3½in (9cm) wide, while the medium roses measure about 1¾in (4.5cm).

MATERIALS

- 7½in (20cm) x 20in (50cm) crepe paper in the following colors:
  White
  Pale Pink
  Pink or Rose
  Mauve
- Matte fabric rose leaves
- Six artificial roses and buds up to 1in (2.5cm) across
- 30in (76.2cm) artificial leafy garland vine
- 18-gauge fabric-covered stem wire
- 30-gauge spool wire
- ½in (12mm)-wide olive green floral tape
- ¼in (6mm)- and ⅜in (1cm)-diameter dowels

YOU'LL ALSO NEED:

large and small petal patterns (see page 120); pliers with wire cutters; access to photocopier; ruler; and scissors.

Instructions

1. Make large rose. Photocopy and cut out large and small petal patterns (see page 120). Cut and layer three 20in (50cm) square sheets of crepe paper so grain runs in same direction. Keeping layers together, cut four 2½in (6.5cm) squares for small petals, five 3½in (9cm) squares for medium petals, and one 6in (15cm) square for large petal. Keeping layers intact, fold each square in half along grainline, hold petal pattern against fold, and cut (see illustration A, facing page). Unfold petals, but do not separate layers.

2. Curl petals. Lay ten petals in a row, smaller petals at left. Pick up first small petal, set ¼in (6mm) dowel on top edge, and roll toward you for two to three revolutions (illustration B). To crimp and set curl, push crepe paper in at each end toward middle (illustration C). Remove dowel and return petal to lineup. Curl second small petal in same way. Curl and crimp remaining two small petals and four of the medium petals diagonally along sides, so curls meet in point at top edge (illustration D). For remaining two petals (one medium and one large), change to ⅜in (1cm) dowel. Curl and crimp diagonal and top edges to form one continuous rounded edge (illustration E).

3. Shape petals. Turn petals over. Using thumb, gently stretch and push out middle of each petal to form bowl-shaped dome (illustration F). For innermost petals (first three in lineup), form

Making the Crepe Paper Roses

A. Cut each petal from a triple layer of crepe paper.

B. Roll the top edge of the small petal around a dowel.

C. Crimp the rolled section to set the curl.

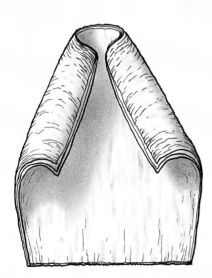

D. Make diagonal curls on the rose's middle petals.

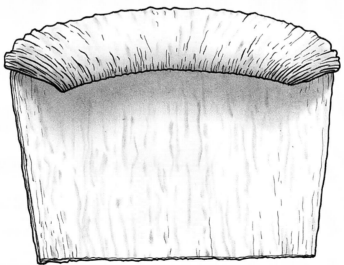

E. Curl the entire top edge on the rose's outer-most petals.

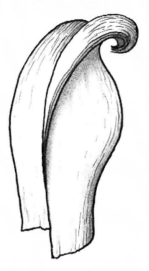

F. Gently stretch the crepe paper to give each petal additional shape.

19

For a holiday version of this garland, mix white crepe paper roses with artificial holiday greens and red berries.

bowl closer to top edge. For outermost petals (last two in lineup), form bowl closer to lower edge.

4. Make rose core. Cut 18in (46cm) length from stem wire, then fold in half. Roll 6in (15cm) square of crepe paper into tube shape, rumpling paper to increase bulk. Center tube within wire fold, fold both tube ends up, and twist wire (illustration G). To form core, fold tube ends back down around twisted wire (illustration H). Wrap base with 30-gauge spool wire, trapping ends in wrapping wire. Twist ends together to form tight, secure bud (illustration I).

5. Add petals to rose. Press smallest petal from lineup against core, opposite crevice. Cup second and third petals around core to fill gaps (illustration J). Bind these three petals to core with spool wire, as in step 4. Stagger additional petals around core, with last two to three (largest) petals higher so edges cup outward. Bind base of rose tightly with spool wire. Wrap floral tape firmly around base and down stem, adding leaf stems as you tape (illustration K).

6. Make medium-size rose. Follow steps 1 through 5 for large rose with following exceptions: Layer two sheets of crepe paper instead of three and use ¼in (6cm) dowel to curl petals (steps 2 and 3). Cut 5in (12.5cm) square for core and 2½in (6.5cm) squares for smaller petals.

7. Assemble garland. To join roses to garland, lay vine flat and arrange roses along length. Intersperse large and medium blooms with small artificial roses and buds. For trailing effect, place some small blooms and buds near ends. Weave stems into vine, then bind with floral tape. Bend rose heads in various directions for naturalistic look. You can make the garland any length desired (ours measures about 30in [76.2cm]). When assembling the garland, use 1–2 large crepe paper roses, 1–2 medium crepe paper roses, and 1 or 2 artificial roses per 12in (30.5cm) of garland.

DESIGNER'S TIPS

To make roses more lifelike, layer three shades of crepe paper for each petal. Mixing and matching the colors can add intensity to the final arrangement.

Make smaller roses for table arrangements or bouquets that will be inspected at close range. Use larger blooms in decorative backdrops for weddings or parties, or on mantels, valances, or curtain tiebacks, where they will be viewed from farther away.

Finishing the Crepe Paper Roses

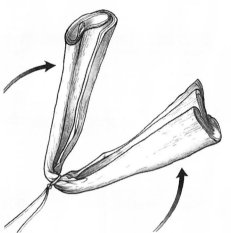

G. To make a rose core, wind the stem wire around center of a crepe paper tube.

H. For a tight bud, wrap the tube ends back down around the wire join.

I. Bind the base of the bud core with wire.

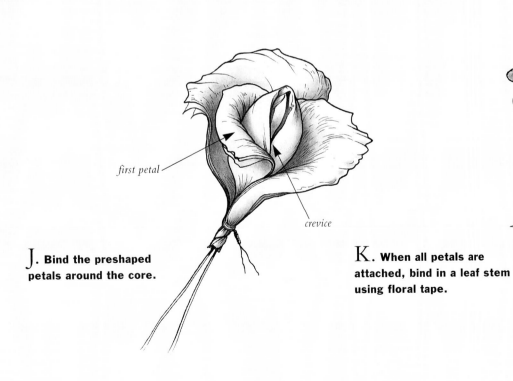

first petal

crevice

J. Bind the preshaped petals around the core.

K. When all petals are attached, bind in a leaf stem using floral tape.

21

Dried Flower Plate Crown

Plate crowns are colorful half-wreaths of decorative foliage that arch around the top of a dinner plate. Similar to a swag, a larger arrangement found above mantels and door frames, the plate crown can be used over and over again, as the base is made of dried eucalyptus and skeletonized leaves. To coordinate the crown with your china, add twists of complementary silk cording and variegated wire-edged ribbon.

———

For a delicate and original variation on the plate crown, insert roses or other fresh flowers into the arch. If using fresh flowers, use a bud water holder to prolong the display life.

MATERIALS

Yields one plate crown

- **Two types of dried eucalyptus, about ten 6in (15cm) to 10in (25cm) branches total**
- **Seven skeletonized leaves, each about 5in (12.5cm) long**
- **2yds (2m) variegated wire-edge ribbon**
- **1yd (1m) twisted silk cord**
- **One 18in (46cm) heavy-gauge wire stem**
- **Green floral wire**
- **Fresh rosebuds**

YOU'LL ALSO NEED:

cellophane tape and wire cutters.

Instructions

1. Make eucalyptus base. Bend 18in (46cm) heavy gauge wire stem to form semicircle-shaped base of plate crown; crown should extend about 4in (10cm) beyond edge of dinner plate or charger. Starting at either end and using two types of eucalyptus, attach five branches with green floral wire to base (see illustration A, facing page). Work toward center of arc to form radial pattern. Repeat on opposite side until eucalyptus base is complete. Wrap midpoint of twisted silk cord around center of arc, then weave cord through eucalyptus branches. Knot ends of cord and unravel remaining 1in (2.5cm). Repeat process to wind 2 yds (2m) wire-edged ribbon through eucalyptus (illustration B). Curl ends of ribbon.

2. Make cone-shaped accents. Roll seven skeletonized leaves into cones (illustration C), then secure base of each cone with cellophane tape. Wire each cone into arc between foliage stems (illustration D).

ABOUT SKELETONIZED LEAVES

Skeletonized leaves, as their name implies, resemble a skeleton of a leaf. To achieve this effect, the leaf pulp is chemically removed, leaving only the underlying network of leaf veins visible. Without the leaf pulp filling in the "body" of the leaf, the veins resemble the silhouette of branches reaching out from the trunk of a tree. Although skeletonized leaves may appear delicate, their fabriclike texture is actually quite sturdy. The leaves can be purchased wherever artificial flowers and foliage are sold.

Making the Plate Crown

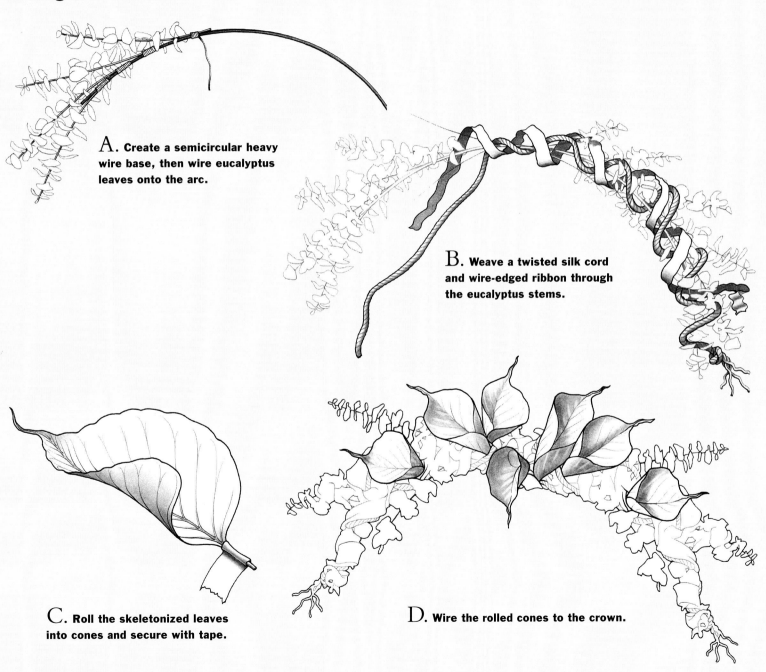

A. Create a semicircular heavy wire base, then wire eucalyptus leaves onto the arc.

B. Weave a twisted silk cord and wire-edged ribbon through the eucalyptus stems.

C. Roll the skeletonized leaves into cones and secure with tape.

D. Wire the rolled cones to the crown.

Copper Wire Garland

This copper leaf-and-berry garland is an interesting departure from the usual dried flower rope. The leaves are made with copper tooling foil, the stems of copper wire, and the berries from beads. Assemble the garland, then don your latex gloves and goggles to apply an antique patina. Once finished, use the garland to entwine your favorite candlesticks, accent a window or mirror, or create a rich centerpiece that will lend a warm glow to your holiday table.

———

This beautiful garland uses copper tooling foil for leaves; such foil is available at craft and hobby shops.

MATERIALS

Yields one 36in (1m) garland

- **12in (30cm) x 12in (30cm) piece copper tooling foil**
- **Eight matte silver ⅝in (16mm) beads**
- **Eight matte gold ⅝in (16mm) beads**
- **Ten shiny silver ⅜in (10mm) beads**
- **20-gauge spooled copper wire**
- **24-gauge spooled copper wire**
- **28-gauge spooled copper wire**
- **Copper polish**
- **Wax-based liquid furniture polish**

YOU'LL ALSO NEED:

copper leaf patterns (see page 120); needle-nose pliers with wire cutters; extra-fine (#0000) steel wool; wooden burnishing tool; 1in (2.5cm)-wide foam brush; small disposable bristle brush; stiff brush for patinating solution; large disposable aluminum pan; denatured alcohol; cotton balls; scissors; fine-point permanent marker; pencil; ruler; tracing paper; clear glue; thin cardboard; computer mousepad; expired credit card; goggles; canvas gloves; and disposable latex gloves.

Instructions

1. Cut out copper leaves. Trace four leaf patterns (see page 120). Glue tracings to cardboard, let dry, and cut out as templates. Using marker, trace six large, six medium, eight small, and six serrated leaves on copper foil. Cut out leaves just inside marked lines. Lay leaves on mousepad and burnish rough-cut edges. Clean leaves with cotton ball moistened in alcohol. Score leaf veins in copper with wooden burnishing tool.

2. Attach stems to leaves. Cut twenty-six 4in (10cm) stems from 20-gauge wire. Using pliers, make right-angle bend ⅜in (1cm) from one end. To crease stem section on leaf, set edge of credit card slightly off-center on leaf and bend foil up toward card. Set wire stem in crease with bent end near top. Lay 28-gauge wire alongside it with its end near bottom of crease (see illustration A, facing page). Use pliers to fold and crimp foil around wires from both sides, then wind 28-gauge wire down around leaf stem in tight spiral (illustration B). Clip off and crimp bent end. Repeat on all remaining leaves.

3. Attach wire stems to beads. For each bead, cut 4in (10cm) stem from 20-gauge wire. Bend wire into loop so it almost touches main stem. Slide bead onto other end (illustration C). Pull wire through hole so double thickness lodges inside (illustration D). If doubled wire is too thick for bead opening, try using 24-gauge wire. If beads feel loose, anchor with dot of glue.

Attaching the Stems

A. **Crease the foil leaf, then set the thick and thin wires against the crease.**

bend end at right angle

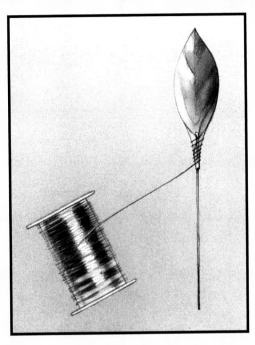

B. **Crimp the foil over the wires, then wind thin wire down around the crimp.**

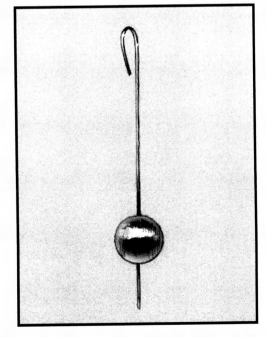

C. **Loop one end of the stem wire, then slide a bead onto the other end.**

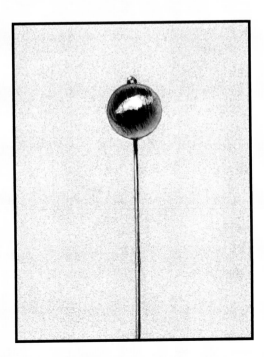

D. **Pull the wire through the hole so the loop lodges inside.**

The copper garland makes a striking centerpiece accent around a bowl or the base of a vase. The garland can also be entwined around a pair of tall candlesticks, draped off a mantel or curtain finial, or used as a curtain tieback.

4. Assemble garland. Arrange beads and leaves in two similar rows so assembled garland will be symmetrical on either side of its center point. Arrange row one right to left, the other left to right, alternating leaves and "berries" for most pleasing effect.

5. Join pieces together. Twist together two small leaf stem wires from left side of lineup for ½in (1cm). Add two small silver berries and continue twisting so all stems travel in same direction. Make sure each stem gets twisted instead of simply spiraling one stem around another (illustration E). To extend garland, unroll few feet of 20-gauge wire from spool and twist in with 20-gauge wire stems. Working from left to right across lineup, add new leaves and berries to garland, spacing them ½in (12mm) to 1½in (3.7cm) apart and twisting their stems and wire together (illustration F). For variation, twist two stems together and then join to wire. Wind together last two leaves from lineup, enclosing spool wire within. Do not cut wire.

6. Add stabilizing wire. Wearing canvas gloves, reinforce garland by winding 20-gauge spool wire back around garland's main stem in reverse spiral to starting point (illustration G). Cut end, bend into loop, and crimp to main stem.

7. Patinate garland. (Always follow manufacturer's directions when working with chemical-based finishes. Make sure area is well-ventilated and wear rubber gloves and goggles.) Scuff copper wires and both sides of each leaf with steel wool, then lay garland in aluminum pan. Separate and flatten leaves, pointing bead wires straight up and out of way. Pour patinating solution into pan. Using foam brush for leaves and bristle brush for wire, apply solution to all surfaces. Dark patina should appear within several minutes. To make patina darker, brush on more solution. When coppery pink sheen disappears into blackened surface, stop patination by washing garland in warm, soapy water, and dry thoroughly. Copper should appear matte gray.

8. Style and burnish leaves. Curl leaf tips by rolling them between forefinger and thumb. To enhance natural look, shape each large leaf so middle swells out and tip curls back. To restore copper highlights, apply copper polish to high points and buff gently; leave low spots and backs of leaves dark. To remove any haze and bring up shine, polish with liquid furniture wax.

DESIGNER'S TIP

Patina solutions do not work instantaneously. The liquid can bead, run off, or dry up, so you may have to rebrush the solution several times. Gently scrubbing the surface beforehand using extra-fine steel wool can speed up the process.

Assembling the Garland

E. **Twist two small, 20-gauge wire leaf stems together, then twist in two berries.**

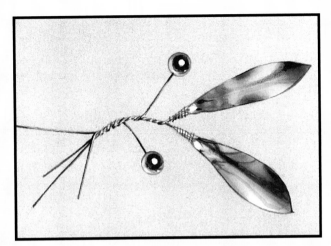

F. **To extend the garland, twist in spooled wire along with the new 20-gauge wire leaf stems.**

G. **To complete the garland, wind the wire back over the main stem in a reverse spiral.**

Quick Gilded Autumn Leaves

Stroll through the woods on a warm fall day and you'll probably wish you could capture the fleeting beauty of the autumn leaves. Here's a quick gilding method that will help preserve the glorious feeling of the season. The secret is to use metallic enamel paint or rubber cement as the adhesive for gilding, instead of the traditional glue, which is called size. Oak and beech leaves are easiest to work with, but most leaves will work well as long as they are fresh.

———

These gold-leaf decorations add a warm touch to tabletops, packages, and wreaths. For a holiday version of this design, substitute gilded holly or ivy leaves.

MATERIALS

- **Two to four dozen autumn leaves in various sizes**
- **One book composition gold leaf**
- **2oz (60ml) container metallic enamel paint or rubber cement**

YOU'LL ALSO NEED:

two ½in (12mm)-wide paint brushes; newspaper or brown kraft paper; and odorless paint thinner.

Instructions

1. Apply size to leaves. Work on newspaper to apply metallic enamel paint or rubber cement to each leaf with paint brush (see illustration A, facing page). Test each leaf for tapelike tackiness: enamel paint reaches correct tack in five minutes; rubber cement, though easier to apply, takes 15 minutes.

2. Apply gold leaf. Once leaves are tacky to touch, press tacky side down onto sheet of gold leaf and rub leaf gently (illustration B). Gently tear leaf from sheet (illustration C). Let leaves dry overnight.

3. Burnish leaves. Dust leaves and leaf edges with dry brush to remove gold leaf flakes and achieve smooth finish (illustration D). Burnishing will add a soft underglow to any areas where the gold leaf has flaked off. Clean brushes with paint thinner.

DESIGNER'S TIP

If you select thin leaves, such as Chinese maple, for this project, be sure to dry them flat in a heavy book before applying enamel paint or rubber cement. This prevents the leaves from curling as they dry.

Gilding the Leaves

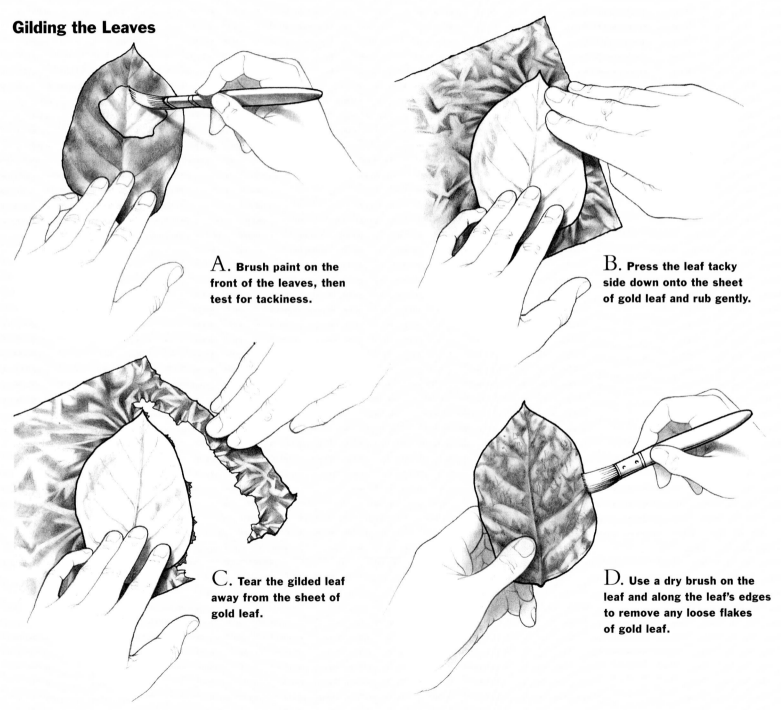

A. Brush paint on the front of the leaves, then test for tackiness.

B. Press the leaf tacky side down onto the sheet of gold leaf and rub gently.

C. Tear the gilded leaf away from the sheet of gold leaf.

D. Use a dry brush on the leaf and along the leaf's edges to remove any loose flakes of gold leaf.

Wheat Sheaf Centerpiece

The wheat sheaf is the traditional talisman of fall, a symbol of all that is bountiful. This wheat-and-rye sheaf centerpiece brings a fall harvest to your dining table. With an ordinary soup can, a hot-glue gun, and some stalks of wheat and rye, you can create this autumn bouquet in less than 30 minutes.

———

For a variation on this design, substitute other autumn grasses and textured ties.

MATERIALS

- **Three packages natural triticum wheat (about 120 stems total)**
- **Three packages rye grain (about 120 stems total)**
- **4oz (120ml) aluminum can**
- **Jumbo braided hair elastic or rubber band**
- **½yd (46cm) waxed string**
- **1yd (1m) 24-strand natural raffia**

YOU'LL ALSO NEED:

scissors or pruning shears; hot-glue gun and glue sticks; ruler or yardstick; pencil; and masking tape.

Instructions

1. Build sheaf base. Open wheat package. Cut 19in (48cm) length masking tape and stick to work surface. Use this to measure, then cut all wheat stems to 19in (48cm). Discard shorter stems. Slip elastic around can, ½in (12mm) from bottom. Insert wheat stems under elastic, lining up snipped ends with bottom of can (see illustration A, facing page). Repeat process to cover entire can.

2. Hot-glue stems. Lay can on side and part adjacent stems below elastic. Apply small dot of hot-glue between stems near base of can. Immediately shift stems back into position over glue and press in place (illustration B). Repeat to glue all stems. Do not remove elastic. Let glue set five minutes.

3. Bind stems at top. Cut ½yd (46cm) length of waxed string in half. Tie one 9in (23cm) length of string around stems, about 4in (10cm) to 5in (12.5cm) below grain heads using half-knot (illustration C). Adjust tension so gathered bouquet core is narrower than can diameter, then finish knot. Trim extra string.

4. Add final layer of stems. Trim rye stems so grain heads fall just below wheat grain heads. Slip rye stems under elastic and hot-glue in place as above (illustration D). Gather rye stems with waxed string and tie. Trim excess string. Stand bouquet upright. Twist 12 strands raffia into rope and tie around bouquet, concealing waxed string. Twist a second rope from remaining 12 strands and use to conceal elastic at bottom of sheaf. Knot both strands at back and trim excess.

DESIGNER'S TIP

To make your own waxed string, cut butcher twine or cotton string to the desired length. Stack two wax blocks in one hand, then slip all but 1in (2.5cm) of string between the blocks. Pressing the blocks together, pull the string through with your free hand to coat.

Making the Centerpiece

A. Slip an elastic band around an aluminum can, then insert the wheat stems under the elastic.

B. Hot-glue the wheat stems to the can.

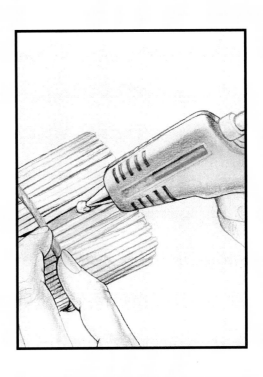

C. Tie off the wheat sheaves about 4in (10cm) from the top of the bouquet using waxed string.

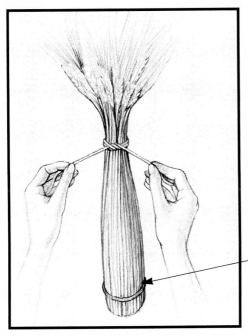

D. Add rye stems to the bouquet, then conceal the string and elastic band with raffia.

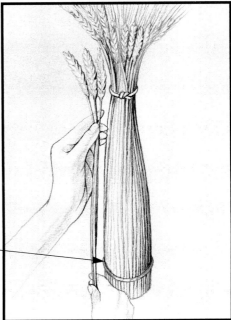

elastic band

Ten-Minute Christmas Crackers

Bring a touch of Great Britain to your table with these quick and easy Christmas cracker party favors, which snap open to reveal small candies, charms, or gifts. All you need to make these festive favors are mailing or toilet tissue tubes, snaps, giftwrap, and double-stick tape. To make the cracker, roll up the snap (a paper strip about 11" (27.9cm) long with a friction cap in the middle that pops when you pull both ends) and a mailing tube in giftwrap. If you pull quickly on the ends of the paper that stick out at each end of the rolled cracker, the snap pulls apart at the middle with a loud pop, in turn tearing the giftwrap at the same location. The cracker (and mailing tube) can then be opened to reveal the candy and gifts.

———

These crackers can be filled with fortunes, candy, charms, or confetti, or small pieces of jewelry. For a variation on the design shown here, wrap the crackers with crepe or tissue paper.

MATERIALS

Yields one cracker

- **Two 1¼in (3.2cm)-diameter x 4¾in (12cm)-long mailing tubes or empty toilet tissue tubes**
- **Snap (available through mail order, stationery supply, or novelty stores)**
- **Giftwrap**
- **½in (1.2cm)-wide ribbon**
- **Gold bullion crimped wire**
- **Confetti, wrapped candy, small prizes, etc.**
- **Double-stick tape**

YOU'LL ALSO NEED:

craft knife; self-healing cutting mat; ruler; small handsaw; serrated knife; cotton string; and pencil.

Instructions

1. Prepare mailing tubes. Using small handsaw or serrated knife, cut one tube in half; set cut halves aside. Remove one end cap from remaining tube, fill tube with confetti, candy, and/or prizes, and replace cap. If using toilet tissue tube, tape over ends with transparent tape. Repeat process for each cracker.

2. Cover tubes with paper. Cut 5in x 12in (12.5cm x 30.5cm) rectangle from giftwrap. On wrong side, mark long edges about 3½in (9cm) in from each short edge. Apply strips of double-sided tape between marks (see illustration A, facing page). Align filled tube on one strip, parallel to and centered along long edge, and press to adhere. Lay snap on giftwrap parallel to tube, red mark on snap facing down. Position cut tube halves at each end of filled tube, then wrap paper around all pieces, trapping snap between layers. Press firmly to seal remaining taped edge. Repeat process for each cracker.

3. Shape and trim crackers. Reposition cut tube halves out about 1in (2.5cm) at each end. Wind cotton string once or twice around unsupported section of giftwrap, taking care not to tear paper, and cinch tightly (illustration B). Remove string. Tie piece of ribbon around each cinched end, as if wrapping a package. Cut twelve 1½in (3.7cm) lengths gold bullion (do not stretch). Stretch one length at midpoint, wrap once around cinched section, and twist ends together to secure. Repeat process to attach six lengths to each end of cracker. Remove cut tube halves (illustration C). Repeat process for each cracker.

DESIGNER'S TIP

You can substitute toilet tissue tubes for mailing tubes. Simply cut the giftwrap about 6in (15cm) longer than the length of the tube and 1in to 2in (2.5cm to 5cm) wider than the tube circumference.

Making the Christmas Crackers

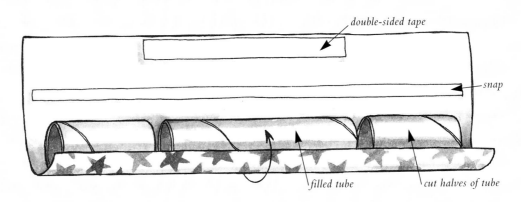

double-sided tape

snap

A. **Roll the giftwrap around the tube and snap.**

filled tube

cut halves of tube

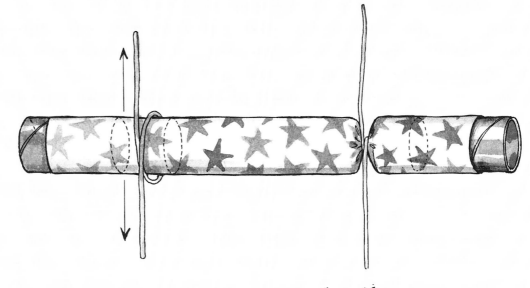

B. **Cinch the ends with cotton string.**

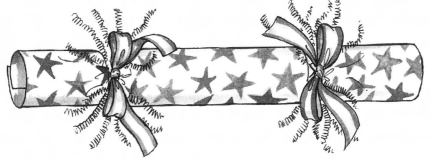

C. **Decorate the ends with ribbon and gold bullion.**

Fresh Flower Topiary

This topiary requires about 40 stems of fresh-cut flowers, which you can purchase at a farmstand or garden center or cut from your own garden. A wide variety of flowers will work well with this design, including but not limited to Cosmos (shown here), Dahlias, Black-Eyed Susan, Carnations, Coreopsis, Shasta Daisy, Marigolds, or the like. For a beautiful Easter centerpiece, use fresh-cut Daffodils and accent the clay pot with a length of sheer, wire-edge ribbon.

———

Watered daily, this live topiary should last for at least a week.

MATERIALS

- **Clay pot, 5½in (14cm) in diameter and 5in (12.5cm) high**
- **Jar or glass to fit inside clay pot**
- **40 flower stems, cut and conditioned**
- **Sphagnum or other dried moss**
- **Several small pieces water-absorbing floral foam**
- **4 to 6 strands raffia**

YOU'LL ALSO NEED:

small, square wooden box (or substitute); ruler; and gardener's shears or other sharp scissors.

DESIGNER'S TIP

The best time to cut blooms is just after the buds have opened and before the pollen sheds. Cut flowers either in the cool of early morning, when the plants' water reserves are high, or in the evening, when their sugar reserves are high. Cut stems about 17in (43cm) long, then strip the leaves off the lower half of the stems.

Instructions

1. Prepare clay pot. Place jar inside pot, then fill jar with water to within 1in (2.5cm) of top. Place small pieces of floral foam around jar to center and secure it inside pot. Gather strands of raffia and knot at both ends.

2. Prepare blooms. Collect stems of flowers together, keeping flower heads level and compact. Add flowers until stem bunch is slightly smaller in diameter than jar. Trim stems even to about 17in (43cm), including blossoms (see illustration A, facing page). To streamline trunk of topiary, strip leaves from lower portion of each stem as necessary.

3. Tie raffia around stems. Wrap raffia twice around bouquet just below flower heads. Lay bouquet over wooden box (or substitute) to protect blossoms, then tie raffia in bow (illustration B).

4. Assemble topiary. Squeeze ends of flower stems together and fit bouquet in jar; bouquet should stand up straight (illustration C). Cover top of pot and around topiary trunk with moss. Water daily by lifting moss slightly and pouring water directly into jar.

Making the Topiary

A. **Assemble the bouquet and trim the ends evenly.**

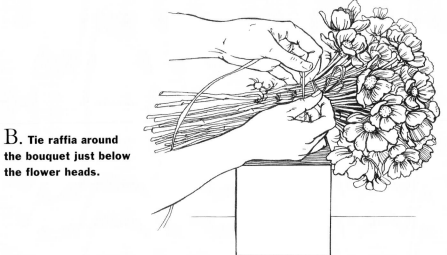

B. **Tie raffia around the bouquet just below the flower heads.**

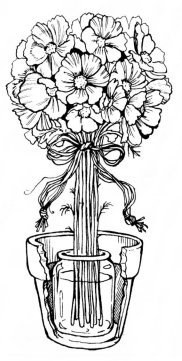

C. **Squeeze the ends of the flower stems together to fit them in the jar.**

Stamped Linen Chair Slip

The rubber-stamped linen chair slip is a printing-and-sewing project that will give your dining area a tasteful lift. Select a rubber stamp with bold, graphic lines that reflects the style of your room. Using washable fabric paint, stamp the image onto two linen dinner napkins. Once the paint is dry, machine-stitch the napkins together on three sides (the unstitched side of the finished cover slips over the back of your chair).

——

When selecting your rubber stamp, look for one with bold graphic lines like this leaf stamp. A delicate image will fade away when viewed at a distance.

MATERIALS

Yields one chair slip

- **Two natural-colored linen dinner napkins**
- **Four ¼in (6mm) round glass beads**
- **Two ¼in (6mm) oval glass beads**
- **Thread to match napkins**
- **Cream heat-set (washable) fabric paint**

YOU'LL ALSO NEED:

leaf rubber stamp; chocolate brown rubber stamp ink pad; brayer; flat pan; white paper; #10 round watercolor brush; pencil and paper; masking tape; sewing machine; iron; press-cloth; rotary cutter; acrylic grid ruler; self-healing cutting mat; tape measure; hand-sewing needle; fabric-marking pencil; pins; button thread, and scissors.

DESIGNER'S TIP

A brayer, which resembles a miniature paint roller, is used to apply ink or paint on a large flat printing surface, such as a linoleum printing block. A brayer features a rubber roller and can range from 2 to 4in (5 to 10cm) in width.

Instructions

1. Printing the leaf border. To determine dimensions for fit, measure around chair back at widest part using tape measure (see illustration A, facing page). If back is curved, hold tape flat against curved area while measuring. Divide by two to determine width of chair slip then add 1in (2.5cm) seam allowance. Measure front and back from top of chair to lower edge of chair back, then add 1in (2.5cm) to 3in (7.5cm) for desired chair slip drop. Jot down measurements, and make sure width of linen napkin is greater than width and thickness of chair back plus seam allowance.

2. Test-stamp border design. On white paper, draw horizontal line equal to chair slip width. Load rubber stamp with brown ink, align it on guideline at left, and press down to test stamp image (illustration B). Lift up stamp, rotate stamp 180°, realign it one space to right, and stamp again (illustration C). Repeat process to fill out border (illustration D). If spacing between leaves pleases you, proceed to step 3. If not, tighten spacing (illustration E). Cut out test border with scissors.

3. Stamp leaf border. Tape linen napkin right side up to flat work surface. Center stamped test border on one hem edge and tape down. Turn flat pan face down. Place small amount cream fabric paint on pan bottom and load brayer by rolling through paint. Shed excess paint by rolling on clean area of pan, then roll brayer across rubber stamp to coat all raised areas. To print bor-

Measuring Your Chair

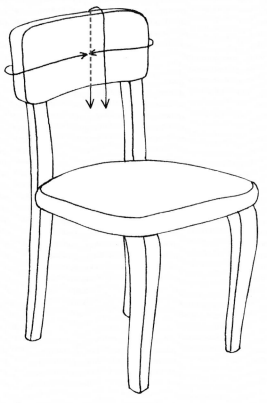

A. **Measure your chair for a custom fit.**

Making Test Prints

B. **Draw a guideline on paper and stamp one test leaf.**

C. **Rotate the stamp 180° and stamp a second leaf.**

D. **Repeat the test border to the end of the guideline.**

E. **If the spacing is too loose, make a new test border with tighter spacing in between the test-stamps.**

51

For a holiday variation on this design, substitute cream-colored linen napkins, silver fabric paint, and gold stamping ink.

der, position stamp so lower edge butts top of hemstitching and side edges line up with test border pencil lines. Gently press down stamp, then lift up. Reload stamp and repeat, rotating stamp ½ turn after each print (illustration F). Tape second napkin to work surface, then mark center of one edge with pin. Load stamp and print single centered image. Wash stamp promptly so paint doesn't set in it. Use watercolor brush and cream paint to touch up images. Let dry one hour.

4. Stamp leaf shadow overlay. To create shadow effect, slide test border ¼in (6mm) to right and retape. Stamp over images with brown ink from pad (illustration G). Print single shadow overlay on second napkin as before (illustration H). Let dry overnight. To set color, press both napkins using presscloth and hot, dry iron.

5. Cut chair slip pieces. Refer to chair slip measurements from "Printing the Leaf Border," step 1. Adjust front and back napkins to center leaf design on lower edge of slip. Using grid ruler and fabric marking pencil, draw three sides of rectangle on each napkin so that rectangle is 1in (2.5cm) wider than chair slip width and longer than chair slip drop. Using rotary cutter, acrylic grid ruler, and cutting mat, cut out both pieces on three sides.

6. Sew seams. Pin pieces together, right sides facing and edges matching, allowing for ½in (12mm) seam allowance. Test fit on chair and adjust as necessary. Machine-stitch raw edges on three sides; leave hemstitched edge open. To box corners, align top and side seams and sew a seam across both on the diagonal, approximately 1in (2.5cm) from point (illustration I and detail). Turn chair slip right side out. Finger-press creases to define boxy shape.

7. Add beads. Cut 6in (15cm) length of button thread. Knot one end, then draw thread into oval bead, lodging knot inside hole. Thread on two round beads, then tack bead strand to lower edge of chair slip at side seam. Repeat at opposite edge (illustration J). Place chair slip over back of chair so single leaf faces seat.

DESIGNER'S TIP

We used linen napkins for this chair slip because linen has a fine, flat weave that works well with rubber stamping. If you substitute another fabric, look for one without a coarse or textured weave.

Printing and Sewing the Chair Slip

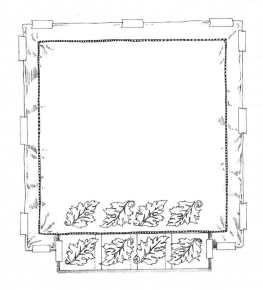

F. Use the test border as a guide for stamping the linen napkin.

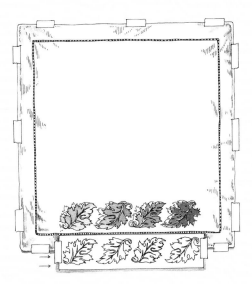

G. Move the guide slightly to the right to print a shadowy overlay.

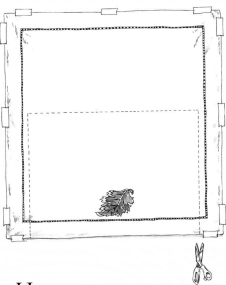

H. Stamp a single motif on the back of the chair slip back, then cut both napkins to size.

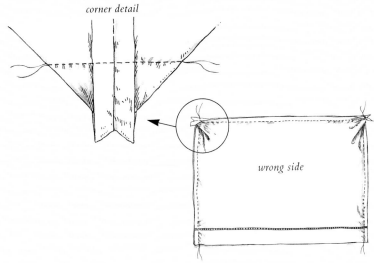

I. Sew the pieces together on three sides and box the corners (see detail).

J. Turn the slip right side out, finger-press the boxy lines, and add beads.

53

Silk Flower Chair Sash

If you love silk flowers and want another place to display them, consider this chair sash, which is designed to accent the back of a kitchen or dining room chair. This sash is made by attaching silk flowers, foliage, and clusters of berries and grapes to a U-shaped wire base. You can fashion a sash to match a decorating scheme or to reflect the season. Celebrate winter with a sash of white flowers and gold or silver fruit, make a springlike mixture of pastels, a fall design with autumnal colors, or a holiday arrangement using rich reds and dark greens.

———

Matching chair sashes will add lively interest to your dining area. These accents can play off your centerpiece or replace it all together.

MATERIALS

Yields one sash

- Eight large artificial flowers (choose three different colors)
- Eight artificial leafy stems with blossoms (such as freesia)
- Six artificial stems with cascades of flowers
- Two long artificial foliage stems, about 27in (70cm) in length and with about twenty-five leaves per stem
- Five artificial berry clusters, assorted sizes
- Three artificial grape clusters
- Two artificial miniature fruits
- 16-gauge stainless-steel wire
- Green floral tape
- Three fabric-covered 18in (46cm) floral stems

YOU'LL ALSO NEED:

wire cutters; ruler or yardstick; pencil; and ribbon or additional fabric-covered stems for attaching sash to chair.

Instructions

1. Make base of sash. Cut two 23in (58cm) lengths of wire. Hold them together, and wrap entire length with floral tape. On flat work surface, bend base into **U** shape about 15in (38cm) across at widest part.

2. Decorate base. Work from ends toward center. Tape two or three cascading stems to each end so blossoms dangle freely (see illustration A, facing page). Wind two long foliage stems around entire length of base, working each one from opposite direction to vary leaf sizes (illustration B).

3. Add large silk flowers. Wind flower stems around base to attach each bloom (illustration C). Fill in remainder of sash with leafy stems containing blossoms (illustration D).

4. Fill in gaps. Wind grape and berry clusters and fruits onto base. To make tendrils, wind floral stems around pencil in tight spirals. Trim spirals to desired length and wind onto base.

5. Attach sash to chair. Make ties of ribbon or use additional fabric-covered floral stems to attach finished sash to chair.

DESIGNER'S TIP

The chair sash can also be used to decorate a mantel or as a centerpiece winding around a pair of candlesticks.

Making the Chair Sash

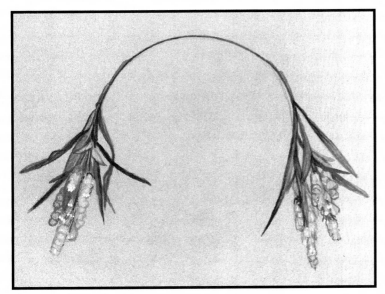

A. Tape two or three cascading stems to each end of a wire base.

B. Wind two long foliage stems around the base.

C. Wind the stems of the large flowers onto the base.

D. Use the grape and berry clusters, fruits, and tendrils to fill the gaps.

table lighting

Curtain Finial Candlestick

A curtain finial, two wooden blocks, and a candle cup are the main ingredients for making this elegant candlestick. For tools you'll need a drill and bits, a small handsaw, a screwdriver, and a small amount of glue. Antique crackle or gold paint or any of the wide variety of paints and patinas are among the many finishing choices.

———

These candlesticks (front to back) were finished with metallic paint that mimics rusted iron, white milk paint, and gold paint.

MATERIALS

- **7in (18cm) wood or resin-cast finial**
- **1³⁄₈in (3.5cm) x 1¹⁄₂in (3.7cm) wood candle cup**
- **Brass insert for candle cup**
- **4¹⁄₂in (11.5cm) square rosette block**
- **3¹⁄₂in (9cm) square fence post baseplate**
- **#10 x 1¹⁄₂in (3.7cm) screw**
- **Wood glue**
- **Paint or finish of choice**
- **Wood putty**

YOU'LL ALSO NEED:

drill and bits; small handsaw; screwdriver; sandpaper; hot-glue gun and glue sticks; ruler; pencil; and small knife.

DESIGNER'S TIP

If excess glue squeezes out of a joint, don't try to wipe it off, as it will interfere with your finish. Instead, let the glue dry and then pick it off with a knife point.

Instructions

1. Make candlestick base. Apply wood glue to top of 4¹⁄₂in (11.5cm) square block and bottom of 3¹⁄₂in (9cm) baseplate. Press glued surfaces together (see illustration A, facing page). Let glue dry 15 minutes.

2. Attach finial to base. Measure and mark center on top of candlestick base (unless it has a predrilled hole). Select bit slightly smaller than diameter of screw on bottom of finial. Drill hole at mark, through baseplate and two-thirds into rosette block. Screw finial into candlestick base until it rests snugly on top block (illustration B). Lightly trace outline of finial on base, then unscrew to apply glue to both parts. Rescrew finial until tight and let glue dry 15 minutes.

3. Attach candle cup. Saw top dome off finial. Sand end lightly. Measure and mark center of sawed end. Using ³⁄₈in (10mm) bit, drill ⁵⁄₈in (16mm)-deep hole at mark. Drive #10 x 1¹⁄₂in (3.7cm) screw through candle cup hole so ¹⁄₄in (6mm) tip emerges inside candle cup, (illustration C); let ¹⁄₂in (12mm) show at bottom. To test-fit candle cup, insert screw head into hole on sawed end of finial until candle cup rests firmly. Drill hole deeper if necessary. Attach candle cup permanently with hot glue.

4. Finish candlestick. Fill any cracks or gaps between joined pieces with putty. Let dry overnight, then sand off excess putty. Apply desired finish following manufacturer's directions and let dry. Install brass candle cup insert; cup will rest on ¹⁄₄in (6mm) tip of screw inside candle cup.

Making the Candlestick

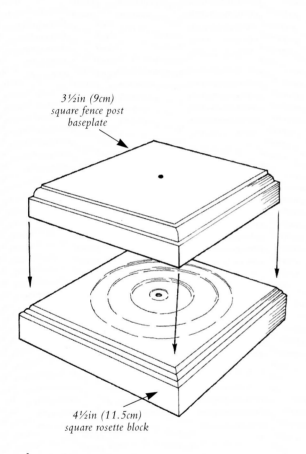

3½in (9cm)
square fence post
baseplate

4½in (11.5cm)
square rosette block

A. **Make a base by gluing a fence post base plate to a rosette block.**

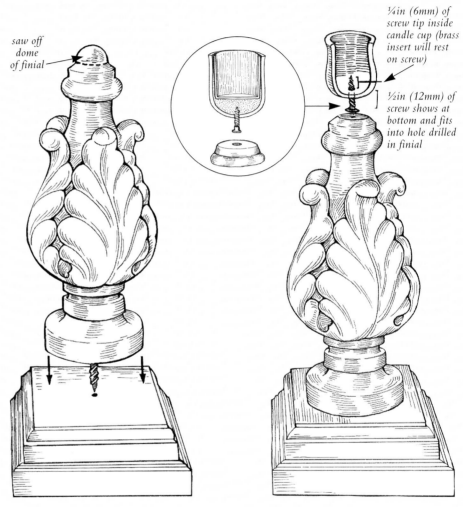

saw off
dome
of finial

¼in (6mm) of
screw tip inside
candle cup (brass
insert will rest
on screw)

½in (12mm) of
screw shows at
bottom and fits
into hole drilled
in finial

B. **Screw the finial into the base, then saw off the top dome.**

C. **Use a screw to lend support, then hot-glue the wood candle cup to the top of the finial.**

Dipped Appliqué Candles

Lighted candles make a gathering special; they set the mood and add warmth to a room. Appliqué candles such as the ones shown here are not only fun and festive to make, but can be tailored for any occasion. Start by applying colored tissue paper cutouts to a plain pillar candle, then dip the candle in melted wax for a final coating. When the candles are lit, the colored tissue shapes on the surface appear to glow from within.

———

To make a number of identical shapes from the same color, layer up to twelve sheets of tissue paper, then cut.

MATERIALS

- **One package (20 sheets) multicolored tissue paper**
- **3in (7.5cm) x 6in (15cm) white dripless paraffin pillar candle(s)**
- **4 blocks (l lb or 400g) household paraffin wax**

YOU'LL ALSO NEED:

stainless-steel roasting pan with rack; disposable foil pan; corncob holders; tissue; odorless paint thinner; sharp scissors; paring knife; flat trivets or large heatproof cutting board for work surface; newspaper; kitchen matches; one each 3in (7.5cm)- and 2in (5cm)-diameter jar lids or bottle caps for cutting doughnut shapes; and rubber gloves.

Instructions

1. Cut tissue paper appliqués. Follow the directions below for cutting the various shapes.

• **Doughnuts and circles:** Cut three 3in (7.5cm) squares of tissue paper and fold in quarters. Hold folded corner against center of 2in (5cm)-diameter jar lid. From tissue paper cut quarter arc following lid edge (see illustration A, facing page). Remove lid, cut second arc about ⅝in (16mm) in from first, and open paper to reveal doughnuts. For smaller doughnuts, repeat using 1¾in (4.5cm) bottle cap. Cut seven ½in (12mm)-diameter circles freehand.

• **Squares:** Cut twelve 1¼in (3.2cm) squares from each of three different colored tissue paper sheets. Repeat to cut ⅝in (16mm) squares and ¼in (6mm) squares.

• **Vertical waves:** Cut five strips measuring 6in (15cm) x 1½in (3.7cm), then cut long edges into wavy curves.

2. Apply tissue shapes to candle. Protect work surface with newspaper. Put on rubber gloves. Moisten small wad of tissue with paint thinner, and rub over candle until entire surface is gummy. Press appliqués onto surface, then rub gently with fingertip (illustration B). Dispose of tissue and store paint thinner before proceeding to next step. Remove rubber gloves.

3. Melt paraffin wax in double boiler. Fill stainless-steel roasting pan halfway with water so rack is covered and set on burner. Set foil pan on rack. Place four paraffin bricks in foil pan. Heat double boiler on low for ten minutes.

4. Roll candle in melted paraffin. Turn off stove. Carefully remove double boiler and set on trivets. Use a kitchen match to heat prongs of corncob holder for few seconds, then push hot prongs into candle near center of base. Repeat at wick end. Hold candle with corncob holders, above melted wax at back of pan. Roll candle forward, skimming across wax surface in one continuous motion. Coat entire surface (illustration C), then quickly hold upright for 30 seconds. Repeat entire rolling sequence, hold upright for one minute, then remove prongs.

5. Finish candle. Place candle on 2in (5cm) jar lid. Immediately smooth any rippling at lower edge with paring knife. Let set five minutes. To smooth over bumps and fill in holes, dip and roll top of candle in liquid wax, then stand candle upright. Let cool at least five minutes before handling.

> ### DESIGNER'S TIP
> For variation on this design, substitute other colors of tissue paper. Gold and red work well for Christmas; pink and blue for a baby shower. When mixing and matching colors, limit the number of colors on one candle to three. More colors become difficult to coordinate.

Making the Candles

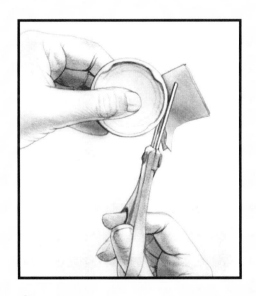

A. Using a jar lid as a guide, cut multiples of doughnut shapes from the colored tissue paper.

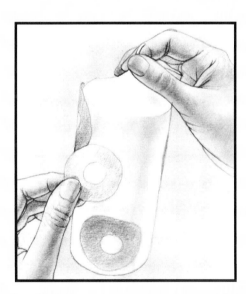

B. Wipe the candle with paint thinner, then arrange the designs on the surface of the candle.

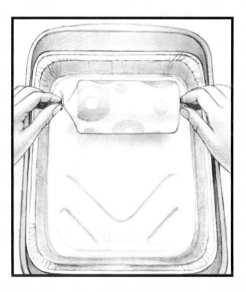

C. Roll the candle in melted wax using one continuous action.

Heirloom Beaded Lampshade

Purchased in a furniture store or a decorator's showroom, a beaded lampshade such as the one shown here might cost $200. You can make your beaded shade, however, for under $50. All you need to get started are a small wire frame shade, fine wire, and an assortment of glass beads.

—

On the lamp shade shown here, the beaded wire strands are pulled fairly taut. For a Victorian look, use a scalloped shade and drape the beaded wire downward. For a vibrant effect, try beads of colored glass instead of gold seed beads.

MATERIALS

- **2in (5cm) x 4in (10cm) x 4in (10cm) wire frame for shade**
- **8oz (225gm) 3/16in (5mm) gold seed beads**
- **About thirty six 3/8in (9mm) magenta beads**
- **Four glass teardrop beads**
- **Two spools 24-gauge wire**

YOU'LL ALSO NEED:

beading pliers and wire cutters.

DESIGNER'S TIP

Once you start winding the beaded wire onto the shade frame, you'll discover that finding the right tension for the wire is critical. If you pull the wire too tight, it will slip upward. If you let it hang too loose, it will sag. Experiment at the start to get it just right.

Instructions

1. String beads on wire. Cut an arm's length of wire. String with gold seed beads. When done, loop both ends of wire so beads don't spill off. Repeat to string all gold seed beads.

2. Wind beaded wire around frame. Wrap one end of one beaded wire strand around spoke at upper rim of shade. Begin winding beaded wire around shade frame (see illustration A, facing page). At each spoke, spread beads to expose wire, then secure to frame by wrapping once. Repeat to cover entire shade (illustration B), ending each strand at spoke. To end off, twist wire tightly around spoke and clip excess.

3. Add beads to bottom rim. Start new wire at one lower corner of shade. String teardrop bead for corner, then alternate seed beads with the larger miracle beads to cover one bottom edge (illustration C). At corner spoke, wrap wire once to secure as in step 2. Then repeat process to add teardrop beads at remaining corners and alternating beads on remaining bottom edges.

4. Cover side spokes. Secure string of seed beads at lower corner (near teardrop), then pull tight to upper corner (illustration D). Wrap once to secure, then reverse direction and pull tight to starting point; secure and trim. Repeat to cover remaining side spokes. Finally, wrap small piece of wire about halfway up each side spoke. Twist and hide these securing wires on inside of shade.

Beading the Lampshade

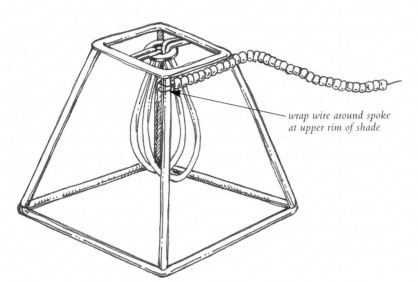

wrap wire around spoke at upper rim of shade

A. **Secure the beaded wire at one spoke, then stretch the beads across to the next spoke.**

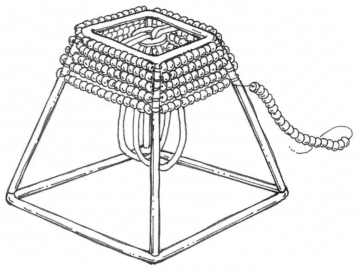

B. **Continue wrapping the shade with beaded wire, winding the wire around each spoke to secure.**

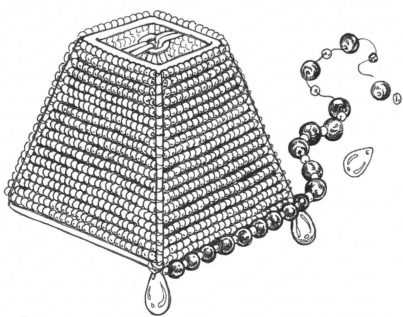

C. **Add a teardrop bead at each corner and a row of alternating large and small beads along the shade's bottom edges.**

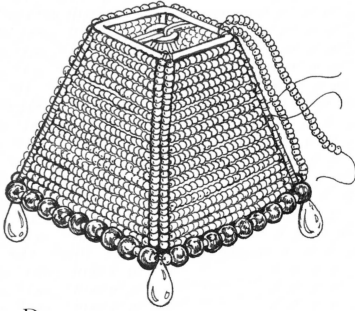

D. **To finish the shade, cover each side spoke with two rows of seed beads.**

Variegated Red Leaf Candleshade

Pair this coppery red candleshade with any yard–sale candlestick and you will have created an elegant accent for your sideboard or mantel. To make the shade, first draft and cut out a template from bristol board, then cover the shade with variegated leaf, a metallic leaf that has been heat treated to create colorful patterns. Once you've assembled the shade, you can use a specialty hole puncher to add coordinating details, such as tiny stars or diamond shapes.

—

To customize this shade design to a specific candlestick, look for hole punchers and deckle-edge scissors with a motif to match the candlestick.

MATERIALS

- **Candle follower and harp**
- **Bristol board**
- **Variegated red copper leaf**
- **Spray adhesive**
- **Shaped hole puncher**

YOU'LL ALSO NEED:

compass or pencil and string; triangle; steel ruler; pencil; scissors; sharp knife; soft cotton cloth; self-healing cutting mat; deckle-edging scissors; two spring-clip clothespins; and two ¾in (2cm) craft sticks

Instructions

1. Draft candleshade pattern. Measure harp height (a), harp width or diameter (b), and bottom diameter of shade (c). Draw vertical line on bristol board and transfer dimensions onto it (see illustration A, facing page). Draw two long straight lines through ends of lines b and c. Label intersection of these lines x. Center compass (or pencil and string) on x and draw arcs e and f through ends of lines b and c (illustration B). Set compass to one-half length of c and mark off three times to either side of vertical line (illustration C). Connect outermost points to x. Finally, add ½in (12mm) seam allowance to one side.

2. Cut out shade. Working on cutting mat, cut out bristol board shade along arcs e and f using sharp knife and steel ruler for straight edges and scissors for curved edges.

3. Apply leaf to shade. Work in well-ventilated space. Spray even coat of adhesive to one side of shade. Let dry until tacky (about ten to fifteen minutes), then press sheet(s) of copper leaf onto adhesive. Burnish lightly with soft cotton cloth, and let dry for one hour (illustration D).

4. Shape and glue shade. Cut two craft sticks to equal shade height. Roll bristol board into shade shape so seam allowance overlaps trimmed edged, hold firmly, and test-fit on follower. Glue overlap, sandwich between sticks, and secure with clothespins (illustration E). Let dry one hour. Place shade under bottom of rounded bowl and weight to set circular shape (illustration F). Let dry overnight.

5. Trim shade. Using deckle-edging scissors, trim top and bottom of shade. Using hand-held star-shaped hole puncher, ring top and bottom edges of shade with star-shaped holes. Space holes about ½in (12mm) to ¾in (18mm) apart at top of shade, and 1in (2.5cm) to 1½in (3.7cm) around bottom.

DESIGNER'S TIP

To safely display a shade on a lit candle, you'll need a candle follower. The follower's ring fits around the burning end of the candle; as the candle burns down, the follower lowers itself along the shaft. The follower's harp has a collar on which the shade rests, lifting it safely above the flame.

collar on which shade rests

ring that fits over candle

Creating the Candleshade

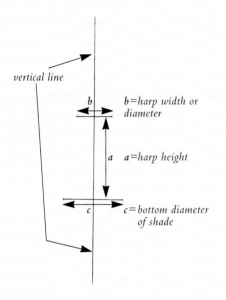

A. To draft the pattern for the candleshade, draw a vertical line. Then draw the harp height (a), the harp width or diameter (b) and the bottom diameter of the shade (c) as shown.

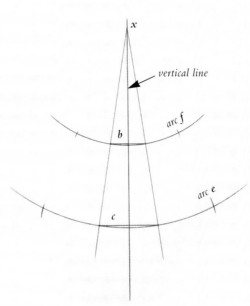

B. Connect the ends of lines b and c to a vertical line, then label the intersection x. Draw arcs e and f with the compass (or pencil and string) centered on x.

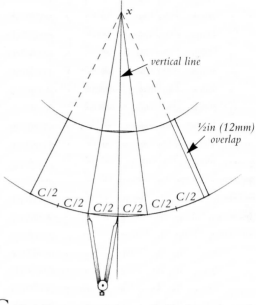

C. Set the compass to one-half of c and mark off three times to either side of the vertical line. Connect the end marks to point x, then add a ½in (12mm) overlap at one side.

Covering the Shade with Leaf

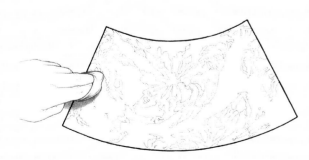

D. Cut out the shade pattern, spray on adhesive, apply the metal leaf, and burnish gently with a soft cotton cloth.

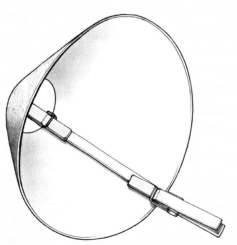

E. Roll the shade, then glue the shade overlap and clamp it between two craft sticks.

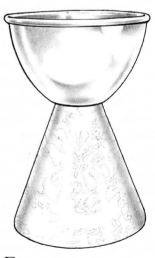

F. Place the shade under a round bowl to set the shape.

75

Decorative Sheet Wax Candles

If you're looking for a simple way to dress up a solid-colored candle, try this cut-and-press technique. Each of the three candles shown here was decorated with designs cut from sheets of honeycomb beeswax. The cut wax images are heated slightly with a blow dryer, then pressed in place. Each candle varies slightly in its level of difficulty. To create the beginner's version, the star candle shown at left, simply cut out shapes using a cookie cutter. The candle decorated with diamonds is slightly more difficult to make as you need to measure and cut squares of wax using a craft knife and grid ruler. For the plaid candle, the most time-consuming of the three, cut a series of horizontal stripes from wax, then fill in the vertical stripes of the pattern with smaller pieces of wax.

—

Each of the candle designs shown here uses the same technique: cut designs from sheet wax, then adhere the designs in place using heat from a blow dryer.

MATERIALS

- **Honeycomb beeswax sheets (assorted colors)**
- **3in (7.5cm)-diameter pillar-style candles**

YOU'LL ALSO NEED:

small star-shaped cookie cutter; can of soup (unopened); hair dryer; craft knife; newsprint; self-healing cutting mat; acrylic grid ruler or straightedge; tape measure; graph paper; pencil; and scissors.

Instructions

Star Candle

1. Cut star appliqués. Lay honeycomb wax on sheet of newsprint. Set star cookie cutter on wax, set can on top, and press down firmly to cut wax clear through (see illustration A, facing page). Gently poke wax star from cutter with fingertip or eraser end of pencil. Repeat process to cut additional stars.

2. Affix stars to candle. Using blow dryer at low setting and holding dryer about 12in (30.5cm) away from stars, heat stars for ten to fifteen seconds, or just enough to make them pliable. Heat candle in same way, for the same amount of time, rotating it with fingers to warm all sides. Briefly reheat stars. Position one star against candle and press gently until adhered. Repeat process for remaining stars (illustration B).

Diamond Candle

1. Determine appliqué area. Measure candle height and circumference. Draft rectangle this size on graph paper for candle template. Cut out template with scissors.

2. Cut diamond appliqués. Divide candle circumference by 4. On new sheet of graph paper, draw one horizontal line this length. Then draw second, vertical perpendicular line, measuring same length, bisecting first line (makes plus sign). Connect ends of lines to make diamond (or square, if turned 45°). This template will be used to cut diamond-shaped pieces of wax. Lay honeycomb wax on sheet of newsprint. Using grid ruler, craft knife, and diamond template drawn above, score four squares this size on wax; complete cuts with scissors. To test-fit squares, arrange them on point in horizontal row across middle of candle graph-paper template (illustration C). If points at each end extend beyond side edges of template, shave all four diamonds to make them slightly smaller. Cut additional squares to corrected size, and continue building diamond pattern until candle template is

Making the Star Candle

A. **To cut through the stiff wax, press on the cookie cutter with a soup can.**

B. **Heat the wax stars with a hair dryer, then press them onto the candle.**

Making the Diamond Candle

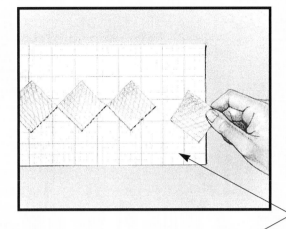

C. **Arrange four wax diamonds across the candle template to check the fit.**

graph paper template

cutting mat

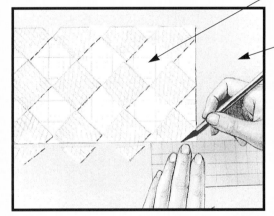

D. **Complete the diamond grid, trimming off the upper and lower edges.**

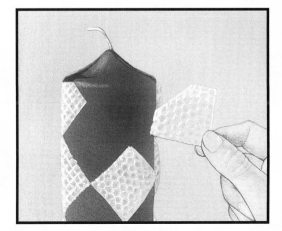

E. **Heat the diamonds, then adhere them to the candle one by one.**

79

For variations on this design, combine smooth sheets of wax with honeycomb wax, or overlap cut motifs to create a two-tone layered effect.

filled. Trim off overhang even with top and bottom edges of template (illustration D).

3. Affix diamonds to candle. Using blow dryer at low setting, heat diamonds ten to fifteen seconds, as with stars; take care not to blow them from their positions. Heat candle in same way, rotating with fingers as you heat it. Position diamonds one at a time and press gently to adhere; complete top row first, then move to second and third horizontal rows. Continue until all remaining pieces are adhered (illustration E).

Plaid Candle

1. Determine appliqué area. Same as diamond candle, step 1. Cut out candle template with scissors.

2. Cut horizontal strips. Place one color of honeycomb wax on sheet of newsprint. Using grid ruler and craft knife, score 1in (2.5cm)-wide strip equal to candle circumference; complete cut with scissors. Repeat process to cut one strip for every 3in (7.5cm) of candle height. Lay strips horizontally on candle template equidistant from each other and from top and bottom edges. From second color of honeycomb wax, cut same number of ⅜in (9mm)-wide strips, plus one extra. Lay second color strip ¼in (6mm) above first color strip; lay extra strip ¼in (6mm) above lower edge (illustration F).

3. Affix horizontal strips to candle. Use blow dryer at low setting to heat candle. Lay candle on side at middle of template and perpendicular to wax strips. Lift wax strips around candle, one at a time, from each side. As each strip comes full circle, trim and butt ends (illustration G).

4. Cut and affix four vertical strips. Score and cut 1in (2.5cm)-wide strip (any length) from second color of honeycomb wax. From this strip, cut a ¼in (6mm) segment to fit space from base of candle to lowest horizontal strip. Heat briefly using blow dryer at low setting, and press into place. Repeat process to adhere a total of four segments equally spaced around candle base. Next, cut four segments to fit space between lowest horizontal strip and strip above it; heat each segment, align with segment placed previously, and press into place. Continue filling gaps between horizontal strips to build four vertical strips from bottom up. To finish plaid, score and cut ⅜in (9mm)-wide strip from first color of wax. Starting at base of candle, cut segments to fit gaps and adhere them ⅜in (9mm) to right of vertical strips (illustration H).

DESIGNER'S TIP

Sheet wax comes in both smooth and honeycomb sheets. The wax cuts easily with a craft knife and ruler or straightedge for geometric designs, scissors for freehand designs, or biscuit and/or cookie cutters for more controlled designs. When working with the sheets of wax, keep your surface clean, as the soft wax picks up dirt and blemishes easily.

Making the Plaid Candle

F. **Position wide and narrow wax strips horizontally on the template.**

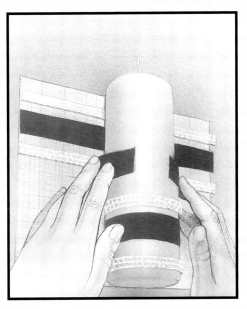

G. **Lift each strip and press in place.**

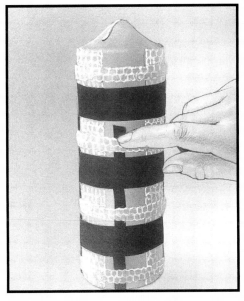

H. **Add the vertical segments of the plaid design one by one.**

DESIGNER'S VARIATION

For another variation on this design, decorate the candle using the wax that is leftover after cutting out the cookie cutter tree shapes.

Votive Candle Townscape

Though this miniature folding screen resembles a complicated woodworking project, it actually requires no heavy-duty tools, nails, or hardware. Instead, the panel is made from balsa wood, which can be cut with a craft knife. The facade is decorated with small scraps of wood and chipboard, which also cover any raw edges on the balsa.

———

To repair small dents, gouges, and holes in balsa before shellacking or painting, mix powdered putty with water, brush it on the blemishes, let dry, and then sand smooth.

MATERIALS

- ¼in x 4in x 36in (6mm x 10cm x 1m) balsa sheet
- ¼in x 6in x 36in (6mm x 15cm x 1m) balsa sheet
- ¼in x ½in x 36in (6mm x 12mm x 1m) balsa strip (for rooftop pieces)
- ⅛in x ¼in x 36in (3mm x 6mm x 1m) balsa strip (for pieces marked "c" on pattern)
- ⅛in x ½in x 36in (3mm x 12mm x 1m) balsa strip (for pieces marked "b" on pattern)
- ⅛in x 13in (3mm x 33cm) strip 1-ply chipboard
- Soft-white acrylic paint
- Spray shellac
- Extra tacky glue

YOU'LL ALSO NEED:

pattern (see page 121); 1in (2.5cm) flat soft-bristle brush; ¼in (6mm) stiff-bristle brush (to apply glue); craft knife; steel ruler; ¼in (6mm)-wide masking tape; self-healing cutting mat; emery board; and spray adhesive.

Instructions

1. Cut house facade. Prepare pattern (see page 121). Work in well-ventilated work space. Apply spray adhesive to wrong side of facade pattern. Adhere pattern on 6in (15cm)-wide balsa sheet. Using craft knife and ruler, cut out facade along solid lines. Cut window openings (solid lines) in same way (see illustration A, facing page). Remove template and set aside. Rub emery board in circular motion over cut edges until wood is smooth.

2. Add window mullions. Using craft knife and ruler, cut several strips from 1-ply chipboard. Referring to template key (a), trim strips to span window openings, plus ⅛in (3mm) on each side. Cut notches in balsa so mullions lie flush with surface (illustration B). Test-fit mullions, then glue in position (illustration C).

3. Add balsa strip details. Lay facade face up. Referring to pattern, cut lengths of ⅛in x ½in (3cm x 12mm) balsa strip and glue to all areas keyed (b). Repeat to cut and glue ⅛in x ¼in (3cm x 6mm) balsa strips to areas keyed (c). Glue horizontal (c) strips first, then vertical strips. To cap roofline, cut sections of ¼in x ½in (6 x 12mm) balsa strip to fit each horizontal surface; cut piece for each roof peak slightly larger, to create slight overhang. Glue down all roof pieces flush with panel back, to create front overhang (illustration D).

4. Cut stand. Cut two pieces of balsa sheet measuring 8½in x 4in x ¼in (21.5cm x 10cm x 6mm). Cut one balsa sheet measuring 8½in x 6in x ¼in (21.5cm x 15cm x 6mm). Mask areas that will receive glue using masking tape: On one 8½in x 6in (21.5cm x 15cm) side of balsa sheet, mask a strip along each long edge. Mask each 8½in x ¼in (21.5cm x 6mm) edge of both 4in (10cm)-wide pieces of balsa sheet. On the back of the windowed panel, mask a strip along each of the vertical edges where the stand will attach.

5. Paint facade parts. Apply two coats shellac to all surfaces; let dry 10 minutes after each coat. Apply two coats white paint to all surfaces; let dry 20 minutes after each coat.

6. Glue stand to facade. Remove masking tape. Glue side panels to back of facade. Glue back panel to side panels (illustration E). Anchor in place with strips of ¼in (6mm) masking tape while glue dries. Use white paint to touch up any uncovered, unpainted areas.

Making the Votive Candle Townscape

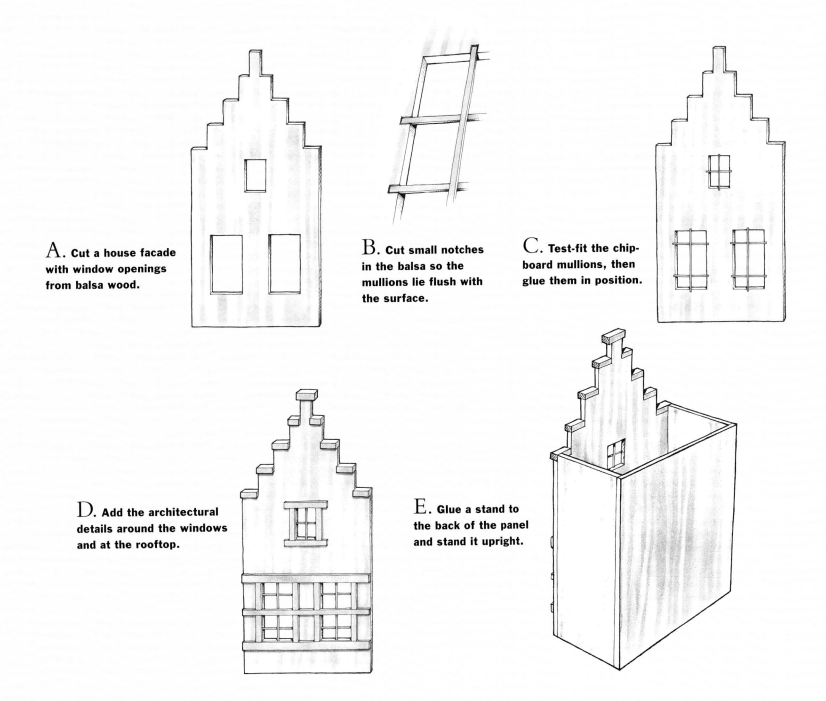

A. Cut a house facade with window openings from balsa wood.

B. Cut small notches in the balsa so the mullions lie flush with the surface.

C. Test-fit the chipboard mullions, then glue them in position.

D. Add the architectural details around the windows and at the rooftop.

E. Glue a stand to the back of the panel and stand it upright.

Mosaic Tile Pillar Candle

You can create this shimmering votive candle shade in a weekend using an ancient mosaic technique that's been updated with modern shortcuts and materials. You'll start by gluing tiny squares of cut glass to a pillar, then fill the space between the squares with tile grout. Cut glass is available wherever stained glass supplies are sold. When a candle inside the pillar is lit, the multicolored tiles cast the light in different directions, and the thin grout lines form a fine web of tracery through which the candle glows.

—

The luminous glow of this hurricane shade is achieved by combining glass tiles of related hues, including gold, honey, amber, brandy, rose, and lavender. For variation on this design, substitute jewel tones.

MATERIALS

- **3½in (9cm)-diameter x 7in (18cm)-high glass pillar**
- **One hundred ¾in (1.8cm)-square precut glass tiles**
- **5-minute epoxy**
- **8oz (225g) ready-mixed tile grout**

For Cutting Tiles:

glass cutter; kerosene; sharpening stone; heavy canvas work gloves; safety goggles; small dish; cotton balls; steel ruler; acrylic grid ruler; graph paper; fine-point permanent marker; and newspaper.

YOU'LL ALSO NEED:

single-edge razor blade; flat, wide stiff-bristle brush; pencil; paper plate; plastic lid; toothpicks; craft sticks; glass cleaner; paper towels; and sponge.

Instructions

Note: If using precut tiles, proceed directly to step 4.

1. Score glass strips. If making your own tiles, use fine-point marker and grid ruler to draft ¾in (1.8cm)-square grid on graph paper. Put on gloves and goggles. Place grid on thick layer of newspaper, then set glass on top, smoother side up, so grid is visible through it. Working in well-ventilated work space, moisten cotton ball with kerosene and set in small dish. Press wheel of glass cutter (see illustration A, facing page) into cotton ball to lubricate, then position wheel on glass ¾in (1.8cm) in from straight edge. Align steel ruler on glass parallel to and about ⅞in (2cm) from straight edge, to butt edge of cutter. To score glass, draw cutter once firmly across surface.

2. Break glass strips. Grip glass on each side of score line between thumb and index finger, and fold each hand into a fist. Rotate both wrists up and out (illustration B). As your thumbs come apart, the glass will snap sharply in two (illustration C). Repeat steps 1 and 2 on remainder of glass. To dull glass edges, run them against sharpening stone.

3. Make tiles. Lay glass strips side by side on grid. Align steel ruler on grid perpendicular to cut edges. Lubricate wheel and score glass surface as before. Repeat process to score perpendicular lines ¾in (1.8cm) apart across all strips. Snap each strip at score lines into individual tiles (illustration D). Repeat for each glass color to make 100 tiles total. File down sharp edges.

4. Glue tiles to pillar. Stand pillar upright on paper plate. Spray with glass cleaner, and wipe clean with paper towel. To maneuver pillar in steps that follow, rotate plate. Count out 13 glass tiles. Following manufacturer's directions, mix small amount epoxy on plastic lid with toothpick. Transfer pea-size glob of epoxy to each tile. Press tiles, one by one, onto pillar around lower edge (illustration E). Before epoxy hardens, adjust tiles so spacing is even. Use toothpick to remove epoxy between tiles.

5. Glue remaining tiles. Repeat step 4 to create even grid pattern (illustration F). Adjust spacing and let epoxy dry. Repeat process to add remaining tiles, for 7 rows total (illustration G).

6. Apply grout. Using brush, work grout into crevices between tiles and along top rim (illustration H). Run craft stick over each crevice to smooth grout. Let grout cure 10 to 15 minutes, then wipe surface of tiles clean with damp sponge. Let cure 1 hour. Run razor blade along top rim to shave off excess grout. Let grout cure at least 48 hours before lighting candle in pillar.

How to Cut Glass Tiles

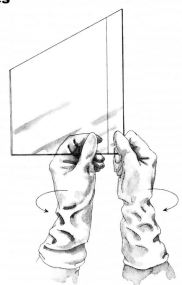

A. **Use a glass cutter with a small rotating wheel to score the glass.**

B. **Grip the glass on each side of the scoreline. As you rotate your wrists . . .**

C. **. . . the glass will snap apart.**

D. **Score and break the strips to make individual tiles.**

Tiling and Grouting the Pillar

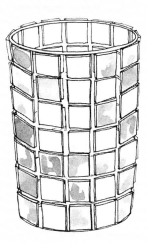

E. **Glue the first course of tiles around the base of the pillar.**

F. **Glue the second course of tiles immediately above the first.**

G. **Continue adding tiles to make an overall grid pattern.**

H. **Work grout into all the crevices, then wipe off the excess.**

89

tableware

Frosted Glassware

This frosting technique is a clever way to transform ordinary glasses or bowls into a gift worthy of a wedding or shower. The secret to frosting is etching cream, a chemical that reacts with glass to leave behind a frosted design. Select glassware that is sleek, simple and transparent, then decide on a pattern. Polka dots and stripes make interesting, contemporary designs, and they're easy to achieve with rubber cement and masking tape. When you're finished, you'll have professional-looking glassware with a personal touch.

—

Glass etching cream and a tape resist allows you to make frosted patterns on glassware. The design can be etched into a clear background or left clear against an etched background.

MATERIALS

- **Assorted colored glassware (such as bowls, plates, pitchers, tumblers, stemware)**
- **Glass etching cream**

YOU'LL ALSO NEED:

rubber cement; ½in (12mm)-wide masking tape; ½in (12mm)-diameter mixing brush; 1in (2.5cm)-wide soft-bristled brush; newspaper; sink; rubber gloves; protective goggles; scissors; small wood blocks; ruler; permanent marker; dishwashing liquid; and disposable glass jar.

DESIGNER'S TIPS

For the best results with etching cream, select plates and bowls that are lightly colored instead of darkly colored or opaque glass or glass with tiny bubbles. This is so the frosted design, which has to be applied to the underside of the glass to prevent contact with food, will be visible through the glass.

For even etching, work as quickly as possible. This way all of the cream can work for approximately the same length of time.

Instructions

1. Practice etching. Before etching colored glassware, practice on disposable glass jar. Frost outer surface only when working with tumblers, goblets, and bowls. On plates and platters, work on underside unless plate is to be used for decoration only. All masked areas will appear clear on final piece and all unmasked areas will be frosted.

2. Mask glassware. To create masks for stripes and dots, press masking tape or brush rubber cement on clean glassware.

• **Frosted horizontal stripes:** Wrap tape once around rim of tumbler, lining up tape edge with rim of glass (see illustration A, facing page). If tumbler is tapered, stretch tape to discourage creases (illustration B). Smooth tape edges with fingernail until well-adhered. If bottom edge has creases or gaps, create new lower edge with overlapping second band of tape (illustration C). Repeat to make striped pattern (illustration D).

• **Vertical stripes:** Mark rim of smaller glassware into fourths; larger pieces into eighths. Cut tape ends cleanly. Align cut ends with rim and press tape down side (illustration E). For broader stripes, overlap tapes (illustration F). Once all vertical stripes are in place, tape rim to protect it from etching cream (illustration G).

• **Clear dots:** Dip mixing brush into rubber cement. Hold brush handle perpendicular to glass surface. Touch bristles down on glass until they fan out slightly, then rotate handle, swirling bristles in circle (illustration H). Press harder to create larger dots. Position dots any way you like (illustration I).

• **Frosted dots:** Make frosted dots like clear dots, but use etching cream instead of rubber cement.

3. Etch glassware. Work in well-ventilated area, and wear long sleeves, gloves, and goggles. Set one piece of glassware on several layers of newspaper next to sink. Prop plates on small wood blocks for easy lifting. Using 1in (2.5cm) brush and working quickly, apply layer of etching cream about ⅛in (3mm) thick to unmasked portions of glassware. Let cream set two to three minutes, then rinse off cream with warm water. Peel off tape and/or rubber cement masks. Wash glass in soapy water and let dry.

Masking the Glass for Frosting

A. **Wrap masking tape around the rim of the glassware.**

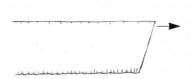

B. **Stretch out the top edge of the tape to hug a tapered glass.**

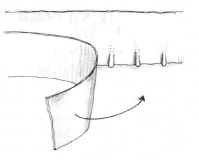

C. **If the bottom edge crinkles, create a new tape edge with a second piece of tape.**

D. **Repeat the process to create additional stripes.**

E. **Align the end of the tape with the bowl's rim, then press the tape in place.**

F. **For wider stripes, cut and apply overlapping tape strips.**

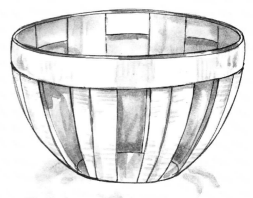

G. **Wrap tape around the glassware's rim to protect it from etching cream.**

H. **Dip a mixing brush in rubber cement, and twirl polka dots on the glass surface.**

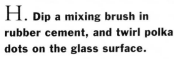

I. **Position additional rubber cement dots randomly.**

Tasseled Napkin Ring

Although this tasseled napkin ring looks sophisticated, its beginnings are actually quite humble. Making a complete set of rings to match your table linens is as easy as silver leafing, or simply painting, several ordinary wooden curtain rings. The tassels are made from skeins of silk and metallic thread. For a finishing touch, we added a miniature picture frame that can personalize the napkin ring or serve as a placecard.

—

For a plumper tassel, add additional skeins of silk-twist thread. For variation on this design, add an assortment of charms to the napkin ring.

MATERIALS

- **One skein (about 15yds or 14m) acid green silk-twist embroidery thread**
- **Wood curtain ring**
- **Miniature picture frame or pewter charm**
- **Quick-dry size**
- **Silver leaf**
- **Clear lacquer spray**
- **Silver spray paint**

YOU'LL ALSO NEED:

¼in (6mm)-wide artist's paintbrush; brown kraft paper; 3in (7.5cm) x 9in (23cm) heavy cardboard; white tacky glue; table knife; soft cloth; ruler; and scissors.

Instructions

1. Prepare ring for leafing. Work in a well-ventilated place. Cover workspace with brown kraft paper. If it exists, remove eye-hook from curtain ring. Lay curtain ring on paper and spray-paint one side. When ring is dry (about ten minutes), paint other side. Add two additional coats, letting dry one-half hour between coats. Apply thin, even coat of size to one side of ring, then let dry until tacky (about 15 minutes).

2. Leaf ring. Moisten blade of table knife by blowing on it, then use blade to move sheet of leaf onto clean kraft paper. Tear leaf into small pieces using perfectly dry fingertips. Pick up leaf with fingertip and tamp in place on side of ring with size (see illustration A, facing page). Repeat to cover one side of ring, then let dry overnight. Repeat process to leaf other side of ring and let dry overnight. Burnish leaf using soft cloth, then seal with clear lacquer.

3. Create tassel. Cut 18in (46cm) length of thread and set aside. Wind remaining thread around cardboard, then gently slide off cardboard (illustration B).

4. Finish napkin ring. Feed one end of tassel loops through center of ring, covering hole created by eyehook (illustration C). Slip loops through second looped end and pull taut to form slip knot (illustration D). Cut loops to create tassel. Affix miniature frame or charm to tassel with glue.

DESIGNER'S TIP

The tasseled napkin ring is an elegant addition to a formal dining table. For a special gift, match the color of the embroidery thread to a color in your china pattern.

Making the Napkin Ring

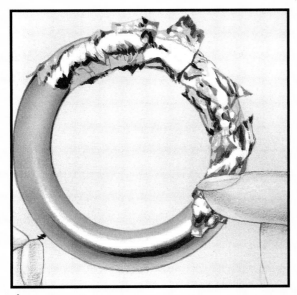

A. Cover the napkin ring with small pieces of silver leaf.

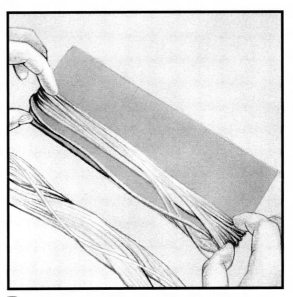

B. Wind the embroidery thread around a piece of cardboard.

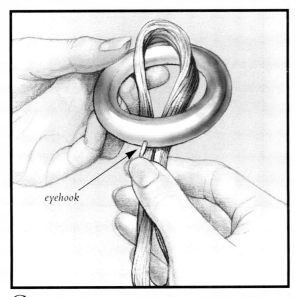

eyehook

C. Feed one end of tassel loops through center of ring.

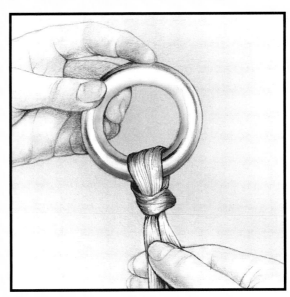

D. Slip loops through second looped end and pull taut to form slip knot.

99

Copper Leaf Napkin Ring

The copper leaf napkin ring is an elegant tabletop accent. Using a quick-gilding technique, miniature oak leaves, pearls, and wire, you can make a set of rings in about two hours. For dressier occasions, use gold or silver leaf instead of copper. You can add your own personal touches, such as small wired acorns or preserved flowers. The copper leaf napkin ring also makes a nice gift.

———

For variations on this design, use silver or gold leaf, greenery like holly or ivy, and beads or berries.

MATERIALS

- ⅝yd (.6m) 1in (2.5cm)-wide copper gauze wire-edged ribbon
- Six 2in (5cm) artificial oak leaves
- Two 1in (2.5cm) gold lamé leaves
- Five ½in (1.2cm) baroque pearls
- Two sheets copper leaf
- 28-gauge spooled copper wire
- 24-gauge spooled copper wire
- Brown floral tape
- Copper metallic enamel paint

YOU'LL ALSO NEED:

newspaper; small paintbrush; soft brush or cotton balls (for burnishing); table knife; scissors; pencil; and needle-nose pliers with wire cutters.

Instructions

1. Apply copper leaf to oak leaves. Cover work surface with newspaper. Using knife, transfer one sheet of copper leaf to work surface. Brush metallic enamel paint on face side of oak leaf, extending paint beyond edges. Immediately press coated oak leaf face down on copper leaf (see illustration A, facing page). Repeat process on remaining oak leaves. Let dry overnight. Gently separate oak leaves, turn over, and remove loose flakes of copper leaf along edges with soft brush. Gently burnish each oak leaf with cotton ball or soft brush.

2. Attach wire stems to leaves. Using 28-gauge wire directly from spool, wind down from base of leaf, enclosing stem and wire in tight spiral (illustration B). Clip wire 4½in (11.5cm) from base of leaf. Repeat to wire remaining copper leaf and gold lamé leaves.

3. Attach stems to pearls. Cut five 5¾in (14.5cm) lengths of 24-gauge wire. Using pliers, bend down one end of wire about one pearl's length, slide pearl onto other end, then pull wire through hole so double thickness lodges inside (illustration C).

4. Assemble bouquet and napkin ring. Gather eight leaf and five pearl stems together in bouquet, then bind with floral tape (illustration D). Wrap ribbon once around rolled napkin and tie single knot. Lay bouquet stem on knot and tie second knot. Fan out leaves and pearls.

DESIGNER'S TIPS

Real oak leaves are too large for a napkin ring. Instead, use burgundy-colored miniature artificial ones. The burgundy color complements the color of the copper leaf and offsets its metallic tone.

You can use rubber cement or size instead of metallic enamel paint, but both these materials take longer to reach their ready (tacky) stages.

Making the Napkin Ring

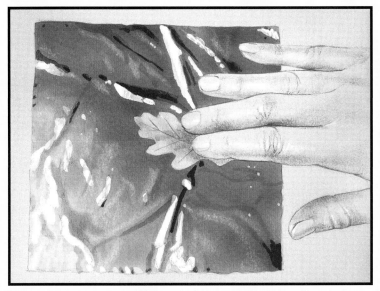

A. Brush an oak leaf with paint, then press it onto a sheet of copper leaf.

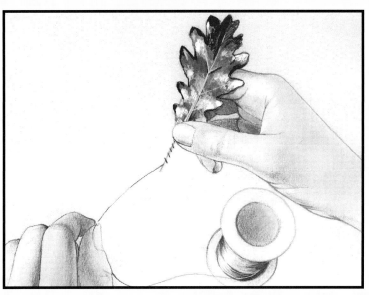

B. Add a long stem to each leaf by spiraling thin wire around the stem.

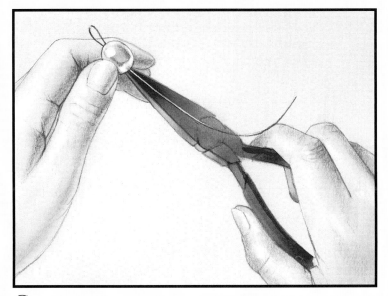

C. Cut a length of wire, bend down the end of the wire, slide the pearl on, and lodge the doubled wire inside the pearl.

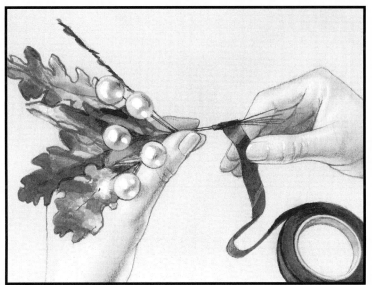

D. Gather the stems into a bouquet and bind with floral tape.

Painted Plates

This hand-painting technique can extend the life of mismatched clear glass plates and bowls and add special plates or glasses to your existing place settings. Start by developing your design ideas on paper. Then, paint your designs on the back of your transparent glassware using china paints. The design must be painted on the underside in order to keep food away from the paint and to make the design more durable, as it should not be scratched. Finally, cure the paint by baking it in your oven.

———

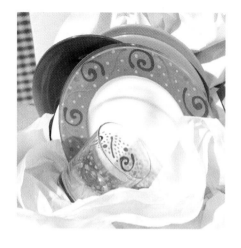

Brightly painted glass plates and matching glassware can spice up a dinner table. This painted plate and matching glass have a contemporary look, but you can make designs to match your decor and personal tastes.

MATERIALS

- **Oven-safe clear glassware**
- **China paints**
- **Cotton swabs**
- **China marker or waxy crayon**
- **Disposable palette**

YOU'LL ALSO NEED:

Soft cloth; window cleaner; scrap paper; dish detergent; towels; oven; and fine-line brush.

DESIGNER'S TIPS

Designs needn't be complex to be effective. Often a streak of color across a surface or a few whimsical shapes are enough to convey a theme.

When painting a flower petal or a leafy fern, create the lines with as few brush strokes as possible, as brush strokes will be visible when the design is viewed from the "right side." Try to create each shape without lifting the brush off the glass. Practice with various paint consistencies on extra glassware.

Instructions

1. Select glassware and paint. Select a paint palette of three or four colors. Create color variations by mixing these colors with each other or by tinting and shading them with white or black paint.

2. Prepare glass surface. Wash glass in warm water and dish detergent to remove grease or fingerprints, then dry thoroughly.

3. Plan layout. Sketch design ideas on paper before committing to glass. Draw final shapes on back of plate or outside of bowl or glass with china marker or waxy crayon. When paint is dry, erase any remaining marks using soft cloth and window cleaner.

4. Paint glass. Paint design in reverse order: Start with foreground or outline colors, followed by subsequent layers. Outline shapes with fine brush (see illustration A, facing page). Let paint dry fifteen minutes between coats. Fill in shapes with paint using brush or cotton swabs (illustration B).

5. Apply background. For opaque background, apply fill color over other shapes using brush or cotton swab (illustration C). Let paint dry completely.

6. Heat-set paint. Let paint dry for 24 hours. Place painted glassware in cold oven. Turn on kitchen vent, or work in well-ventilated kitchen. Set oven temperature at 325°F (165°C) and bake for 35 minutes. Turn oven off and let glass cool before removing from oven.

Painting the Plates

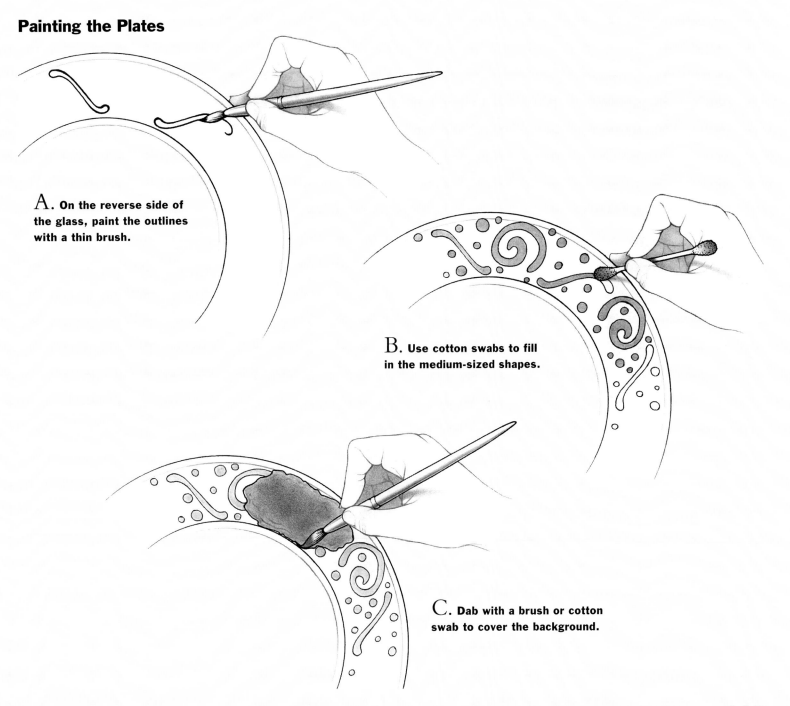

A. On the reverse side of the glass, paint the outlines with a thin brush.

B. Use cotton swabs to fill in the medium-sized shapes.

C. Dab with a brush or cotton swab to cover the background.

Frosted Glitter Glasses

This project uses ordinary craft materials to add a sparkling, frosted decorative finish to the outside of a set of glasses. Start by combining microfine glitter and epoxy glue, which, when applied to the glass, produce a sparkling surface that looks like it has been heat-fused. Then finish the design with frosted effects using glass etching cream.

———

Although the bond created with epoxy is superior to many other adhesives, these glasses should not be washed in the dishwasher. Instead, wash the glasses by hand.

MATERIALS

- **Glasses**
- **Silver micro-fine glitter**
- **Glass etching cream**
- **Five-minute epoxy**

YOU'LL ALSO NEED:

2in x 4in (5cm x 10cm) self-adhesive labels; ¼in (6mm)-wide masking tape; ½in (1.2cm)-wide masking tape; 1in (2.5cm) foam brush; rubber gloves; protective goggles; canvas gloves; rubbing alcohol; craft knife; newspaper; cotton balls; flat toothpicks; disposable plastic lids; and credit card.

Instructions

1. Define etching area. Clean outside of glass using cotton ball and alcohol. Wrap ½in (1.2cm)-wide masking tape around rim of glass; apply ¼in (6mm)-wide masking tape over crinkled edge to smooth line. Mask stripe on stem 1in (2.5cm) below bowl. To ensure tight seal, press down all edges with credit card.

2. Make square masks. Working freehand, use craft knife to score ¼in (6mm) to 1¼in (3.2cm) squares across self-adhesive labels; score a smaller square inside each large square. Turn glass upside down on clean paper. One by one, remove solid and

"doughnut" squares from backing and adhere at random to outside bowl of glass (see illustration A, facing page). Press all edges with credit card.

3. Etch glassware. Put on rubber gloves and safety goggles. Following manufacturer's instructions, use foam brush to apply etching cream to outside bowl between rim and stem masking tape. Repeat for each glass. Let cream set three to five minutes, then wash off cream and remove tape to reveal etched design (illustration B). Wash glasses in soapy water and dry thoroughly.

4. Apply masks for glitter borders. For each etched doughnut, cut self-adhesive square slightly smaller and press into place. Lay strip of ¼in (6mm)-wide masking tape parallel to square edge, allowing small gap; fold end of strip back on itself to make tab. Similarly place additional strips along remaining three sides to complete square border mask. Repeat process for each cutout square (illustration C).

5. Apply ring masks to stem. Wrap ¼in (6mm) tape once around base of glassware stem; fold end of strip back on itself to make tab. Wrap parallel strip ¼in (6mm) away for glitter ring. Mask two more rings near bowl of glass in same way.

6. Apply glitter to border and ring areas. Put on canvas gloves. Following manufacturer's instructions and using toothpick, mix small amount epoxy on plastic lid. Stir in equal amount silver glitter. Using clean toothpick, spread thin layer glitter/epoxy mixture onto unmasked areas bordering squares and stem rings. Work quickly, mixing more glue and glitter as needed. As each glitter border is completed, remove tape. Set aside 1 hour to cure (illustration D). Remove tape.

Decorating the Glasses

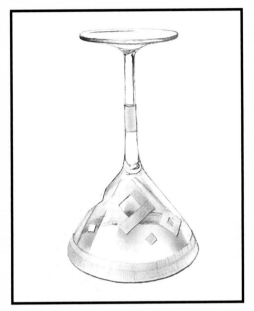

A. **Mask a design using self-adhesive squares.**

B. **Etch the glass to make the design permanent.**

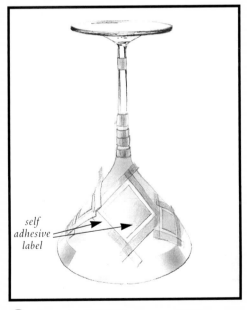

self adhesive label

C. **Mask the edges of each large square . . .**

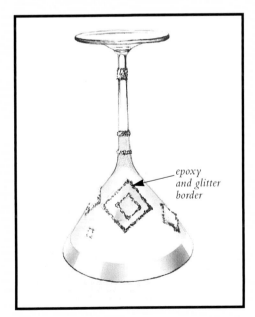

epoxy and glitter border

D. **. . . to add an epoxy and glitter border.**

Stamped Copper Leaf Charger

Personalize your table setting with this decorative glass charger, designed to sit beneath an appetizer, salad, or dessert plate. Using a rubber stamp, copper leaf, and transparent glass paint, you can make unique platters that will dazzle your guests. The design on this charger was placed around the edges of the underside of the dish because only the edges of the charger are visible once the dinner plate is placed on top. In the photo shown here, the dinner plate features a blueberry design that complements the charger's decorative design.

———

The rim of this gilded charger was made with a geometrically-styled rubber stamp. Try finding rubber stamps with holly leaves and berries or fruits and nuts to add a seasonal theme to your creations.

MATERIALS

- **Clear glass dinner chargers**
- **Rubber stamps**
- **Gold size**
- **Copper leaf**
- **Transparent glass paint, cobalt blue**

YOU'LL ALSO NEED:

mineral spirits; soft-bristled brushes; window cleaner; paper towels; straight razor blade; poster board; metal straight edge; pencils; ink pad; compass; and 45° triangle.

DESIGNER'S TIP

If you are unfamiliar with the drying times of varnish, you may want to stamp an extra symbol or two onto your test plate at the same time you're stamping your real plate. That way you can check, with your fingertips, that the size has reached the correct tack without actually touching the project.

Instructions

1. Make template. Create template for transferring designs to chargers. Invert charger onto clean poster board and trace outline. For exact, precise designs, such as the one shown here, find center of plate using illustrations A and B, facing page. Thinking of traced poster board as a clock face, test design by rubber stamping largest design at twelve, three, six, and nine o'clock. Then stamp smaller designs in between large ones (illustration C). Adjust stamps as necessary, creating additional circular poster board templates if desired. For more random designs, proceed as desired to create template on plate backside.

2. Stamp plate. Remove all labels, glues, fingerprints, and oils from plate. Set charger face down on traced poster board template and tape in place. Brush even coat of gold size on face of larger rubber stamp. Carefully stamp size on plate backside over one template location, taking care not to let stamp slip or slide. To correct mistakes, clean with mineral spirits, dry, and begin again. Stamp gold size at all template locations, and let dry until tacky (15 to 30 minutes).

3. Apply copper leaf. When size is tacky, cut sheet of copper leaf into four pieces using a sharp knife or razor blade. Apply one piece of leaf over each sized stamp, tamp lightly with soft clean cloth, then gently buff away excess leaf until clean image appears (illustration D). To correct errors, scrape leaf off with razor blade, wipe with mineral spirits, and reapply. Let dry overnight.

4. Back-paint rim. Brush cobalt blue glass paint on underside of charger rim, covering copper leaf (illustration E). Stop paint where bottom of charger begins. Let paint dry following manufacturer's instructions.

Finding the Center of the Charger

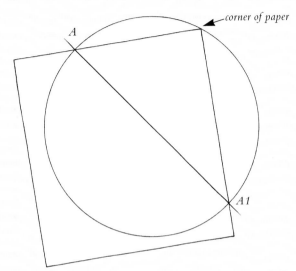

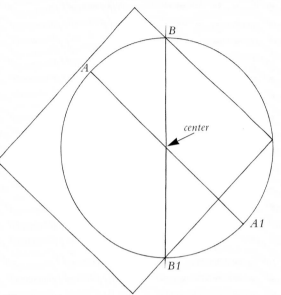

A. To find the center of the charger, place a corner of paper on the edge of the circular template. Mark points **A** and **A1** where the edges of the paper cross the circle, then connect these points.

B. Rotate the paper as shown above and repeat the process. Connect points **B** and **B1** as before. The two resulting lines will intersect at the center of the circle. Use this point to divide the template into eighths.

Decorating the Charger

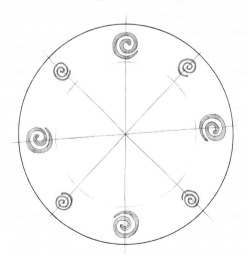

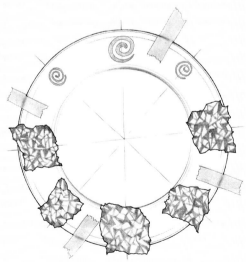

C. Stamp the designs on to the paper template.

D. Set charger face down on template and tape in place. Stamp over all template locations and let dry until tacky. Apply copper leaf over each sized stamp.

E. Back-paint the rim of the charger with cobalt blue glass paint.

Fresh-Flower China

Bring the vivid palette of nature to the table with your own floral china patterns. Start by arranging fresh flowers on a glass plate, then stack a second clear glass plate on top of the decorated plate to hold the flowers in place. You can tailor the colors and textures of the flowers to the formality of your event, match them to your centerpiece, or coordinate them with other florals around your home.

———

For a casual china pattern, randomly cluster the blossoms. For a more formal pattern, arrange the flowers and leaves like hours on the face of a clock. For variation on this design, substitute ferns, ivy leaves, ornamental grasses, a confetti of chrysanthemum petals, or colorful fall foliage.

MATERIALS

- Two clear glass chargers or oversized dinner plates
- Assortment of flowers and greens that will flatten easily (e.g., freesia, phlox, daisies, sweetpeas, holly leaves, etc.)

Instructions

1. Choose plates and flowers. Select fresh blossoms and greens from florist or from your garden.

2. Position flowers. Place lower platter on work surface. Peel back one petal to reveal inner blossom (see illustration A). Position flowers one by one around rim (illustration B). Snip blooms close to base. Flatten each blossom with fingertip.

3. Fill out pattern. Position freesia buds and holly leaves. Conceal snipped edges of leaves under blossoms. Fill out the design with phlox blossoms, daisy petals, and sweetpea blossoms. Lower second platter into position, pressing flowers flat without shifting them (illustration C).

118

Arranging the Flowers

A. **Peel back one petal to reveal the inner blossom. Gently flatten the flower.**

B. **Arrange fresh flowers and leaves on a glass charger.**

C. **Lower the second platter in place, pressing the flowers flat.**

appendix

Patterns

Copper Wire Garland (page 26)

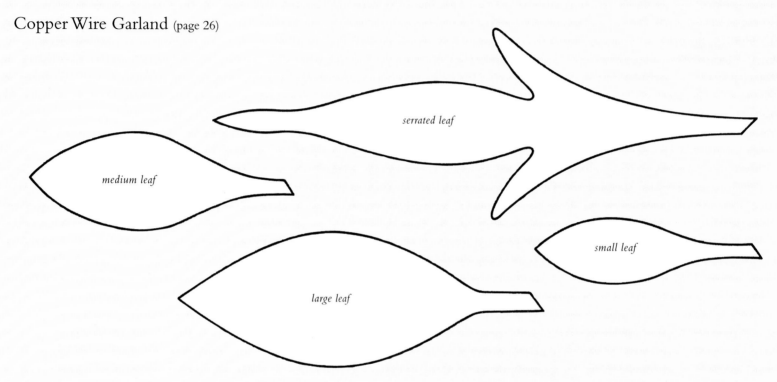

serrated leaf

medium leaf

small leaf

large leaf

Rose Blossom Garland (page 16)

PHOTOCOPY BOTH PIECES FOR THIS PROJECT AT 100%

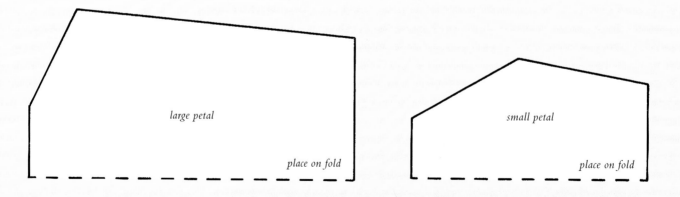

large petal

place on fold

small petal

place on fold

Votive Candle Townscape (page 82)
PHOTOCOPY THIS PATTERN AT 200%

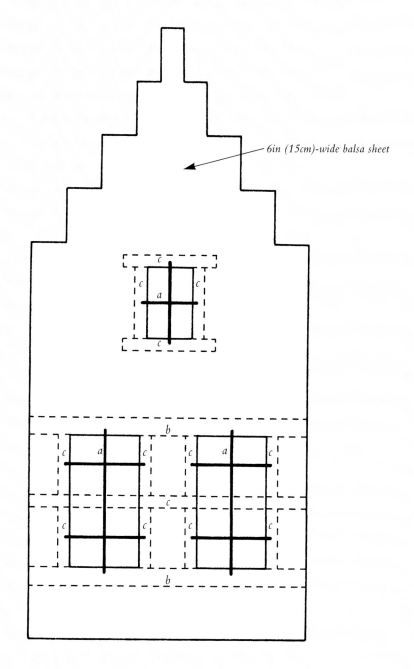

6in (15cm)-wide balsa sheet

TEMPLATE KEY

a = 1-ply chipboard

b = ⅛ x ½in (3.2 x 12.7mm) balsa

c = ¼ x ½in (6.4 x 12.7mm) balsa

Sources

Art Supplies

Artists' Emporium
106-1135 64th Avenue SE
Calgary, AB T3H 2J7
403-255-2090 800-661-8341

Canal Surplus
363 Canal Street
New York, NY 10013
212-966-3275

Coffee Break Designs
P.O. Box 34281
Indianapolis, IN 46234
317-290-1542

Co-op Artists' Materials
P.O. Box 53097
Atlanta, GA 30355
800-877-3242

Curry's Art Store Ltd.
490 Yonge Street
Toronto, ON M4Y 1X5
416-967-6666

Daniel Smith
4150 First Avenue South
Seattle, WA 98124-5568
800-426-6740

Dick Blick Art Materials
P.O. Box 1267
Galesburg, IL 61402-1267
800-447-8192

Gemst Inc.
5380 Sherbrooke West
Montreal, QC H4V 1V6
514-488-5104

Impress
120 Andover Park East
Tukwila, WA 98188
206-901-9101

Jerry's Artarama
5325 Departure Drive
Raleigh, NC 27616
800-827-8478

Mountaintop Mosaic
P.O. Box 653
Castleton, VT 05735
800-564-4980

Ott's Discount Art Supply
102 Hungate Drive
Greenville, NC 27858
800-356-3289

Pearl Paint Company, Inc.
308 Canal Street
New York, NY 10003
800-451-7327 (catalog)
800-221-6845 x2297 (main store)

Reid's Art Material Ltd.
5847 Victoria Drive
Vancouver, BC V5P 3W5
604-321-9615

Texas Art Supply
P.O. Box 66328
Houston, TX 77266-6328
800-888-9278

Beads, etc.

The Bead Emporium
368 Victoria
Westmount, QC H3Z 2N4
514-486-6425

Beadworks
149 Water Street
Norwalk, CT 06854
800-232-3761

Bouclair
1233 Donald Street
Ottawa, ON K1J 8W3
613-744-3982

Creative Beginnings
475 Morro Bay Boulevard
Morro Bay, CA 93442
800-367-1739

Ornamental Resources, Inc.
P.O. Box 3010
1427 Miner Street
Idaho Springs, CO 80452
800-876-6762

Candle Making

Alberta Beeswax and Candlemaking Supplies
10611 170th Street
Edmonton, AB T5P 4W2
403-413-0350

The Barker Company
15106 10th Avenue S.W.
Seattle, WA 98166
800-543-0601

Pourette Candle Making Supplies
1418 N.W. 53rd
Seattle, WA 98115
800-888-9425

General Craft Supplies

Craft King
P.O. Box 90637
Lakeland, FL 33804
800-769-9494

Earth Guild
33 Haywood Street
Asheville, NC 28801
800-327-8448

Enterprise Art
P.O. Box 2918
Largo, FL 34648
800-366-2218

LewisCraft
477 Paul Street
Moncton, NB E1A 5R4
506-857-9585

Loomis and Toles
963 Eglinton Avenue East
Toronto, ON M4G 4B5
416-423-9300

Munro Corporation
3954 W. 12 Mile Road
Berkley, MI 48072
800-638-0543

Nasco Arts & Crafts
901 Janesville Avenue
Fort Atkinson, WI 53538-0901
800-558-9595

National Artcraft Company
7996 Darrow Road
Twinsburg, OH 44087
800-793-0152

S&S Worldwide
6576A I-85 Court
Norcross, GA 30093-1178
800-701-0903

Sax Arts & Crafts
P.O. Box 510710
New Berlin, WI 53151-0710
800-558-6696

Sunshine Discount Crafts
P.O. Box 301
Largo, FL 34649-0301
800-729-2878

Specialty Craft Supplies

The Lamp Shop
P.O. Box 3606
Concord, NH 03302-3606
603-224-1603

Metalliferous
34 West 46th Street
New York, NY 10036
212-944-0909

Viking Woodcrafts
1317 8th Street S.E.
Waseca, MN 56093
800-328-0116

A World of Plenty
P.O. Box 1153
Hermantown, MN 55810-9724
218-729-6761

Glass Products/ Supplies

Eastern Art Glass
P.O. Box 341
Wyckoff, NJ 07481
800-872-3458

IKEA (Catalog Department)
185 Discovery Street
Colmar, PA 18915
800-434-4532

Pottery Barn
100 North Point Street
San Francisco, CA 94133
800-922-9934

Floral Supplies

Blossoms Up
168 Queen St. S.
Mississauga, ON L5M 1K8
905-813-76324

J&T Imports Dried Flowers
143 South Cedros #F
Solana Beach, CA 92075
619-481-9781

White Flower Farm
P.O. Box 50
Litchfield, CT 06759-0050
203-496-9600

Metric Conversions

ENGLISH EQUIVALENTS

$\frac{1}{16}$in = 2mm

$\frac{1}{8}$in = 3mm

$\frac{3}{16}$in = 5mm or 0.5cm

$\frac{1}{4}$in = 6mm

$\frac{3}{8}$in = 9.5mm or 0.9cm

$\frac{1}{2}$in = 12mm or 1.2cm

$\frac{5}{8}$in = 16mm or 1.6cm

$\frac{3}{4}$in = 18mm or 1.8cm

$\frac{7}{8}$in = 22mm or 2.2cm

1in = 2.5cm

2in = 5cm

3in = 7.5cm

4in = 10cm

5in = 12.5cm

6in = 15cm

7in = 18cm

8in = 20.5cm

9in = 23cm

10in = 25cm

1 qt = .95L

1 pint = .47L

½ cup = 120ml

1 cup = .24L

3 lb = 1.36kg

1 fluid oz = 30ml

English System to Metric

TO CHANGE:	INTO:	MULTIPLY BY:
Inches	Millimeters	25.4
Inches	Centimeters	2.54
Feet	Meters	0.305
Yards	Meters	0.914
Pints	Liters	0.473
Quarts	Liters	0.946
Gallons	Liters	3.78
Ounces	Grams	28.4
Pounds	Kilograms	0.454

Metric to English System

TO CHANGE:	INTO:	MULTIPLY BY:
Millimeters	Inches	0.039
Centimeters	Inches	0.394
Meters	Feet	3.28
Meters	Yards	1.09
Liters	Pints	2.11
Liters	Quarts	1.06
Liters	Gallons	0.264
Grams	Ounces	0.035
Kilograms	Pounds	2.2

Credits

All color photography: Carl Tremblay, except Quick Gilded Autumn Leaves (page 32) by Stephen Mays and Fresh-Flower Topiary (page 44) by Bruce Landis.

All styling: Ritch Holben.

All patterns: (Pages 120-121) by Roberta Frauwirth.

Acknowledgments

A collection of this scope requires the talents of many people. Generous thanks to those at *Handcraft Illustrated* who assisted in its preparation: for their creative and technical acumen, senior editor Michio Ryan and directions editor Candie Frankel; for designing and testing many of the beautiful projects, art director Elaine Hackney, photographer Carl Tremblay, and stylist Ritch Holben; for managing a wide variety of odds and ends, editorial assistant Melissa Nachatelo; for intelligent and seamless project management and manuscript magic, corporate managing editor Barbara Bourassa, and finally, to Christopher Kimball, publisher of *Handcraft Illustrated*, whose original vision informed the work on all levels. Thanks also to Angela Miller and Coleen O'Shea, of The Miller Agency, who believed in the project and gathered this creative team together.

About *Handcraft Illustrated*

Handcraft Illustrated is a sophisticated, yet accessible how-to magazine featuring craft and home decorating projects. Each 52-page quarterly issue includes approximately 40 different projects. The projects are accompanied by a full-color photograph, a complete materials list, precise step-by-step directions, and concise hand-drawn illustrations. All projects featured in the magazine are fully tested to ensure that the readers can make the designer-quality craft and home decorating projects at home.

Special departments include Quick Tips, an ongoing series of professional craft secrets, shortcuts, and techniques; Notes from Readers, providing detailed answers to readers' problems; Quick Home Accents, a unique pairing of materials and accessories designed to spur creative craft or decorating solutions; The Perfect Gift, offering creative solutions for designing, making, and packaging your own unique gifts; Quick Projects, a series of "theme-and-variation" projects featuring four to six versions of one beautiful but easy-to-make craft; and Sources and Resources, a retail and mail-order directory for locating materials and supplies used in the issue.

For a free trial issue of *Handcraft Illustrated,* phone 800-933-4447.

Index